"C" Edition

YOUR FIRST FAKE BOOK

Featuring Large Music Notation, Lyrics & Simplified Harmonies

✓ **W9-CLD-472**

Over 100 Songs | **YOUR** | In the Key of "C"

FIRST FAKE BOOK

For Keyboard, Vocal, Guitar and all "C" Instruments

Standards, Love Songs, Beatles' Songs, Rock 'n' Roll, Broadway Songs, Movie Songs, Traditional Songs

Arranged by Alexander Citron

ISBN 0-7935-8503-1

HAL•LEONARD® CORPORATION

7777 W. BLUEMOUND RD. P.O. BOX 13819 MILWAUKEE, WI 53213

Visit Hal Leonard Online at
www.halleonard.com

"C" Edition

YOUR FIRST FAKE BOOK

CONTENTS

INTRODUCTION

A fake book, or lead sheet, is one of the most useful tools for musicians, amateur and professional alike. A fake book has just a single line of music, similar to the right hand in standard piano music. To make it even simpler, there is only one note at a time, representing the melody of a song. If you ever struggled with playing two hands together, reading the two staves simultaneously, you can rest assured that your task here will be easy by comparison.

You will also notice symbols consisting of letters and numbers above the musical notes, such as Cm, B7, etc. These symbols provide flexible guidelines for creating chords, leaving you the freedom to play in whatever style, at whatever level of difficulty you like.

Despite its simplicity, a fake book allows for unlimited complexity and musical creativity. Don't let the name fool you. A fake book is so called because the performer improvises or "fakes" the chords and accompaniment. Yet, despite the name, this is a "real" musical experience, mastered by Mozart, Beethoven and countless others — in fact, some of their greatest compositions were improvised or "faked" and then written down.

Why the FIRST Fake Book?

Although the layout is simple, playing using a fake book to its maximum advantage takes a high degree of skill. Many of the fake books commercially available are designed for experienced musicians. The beginner may find that even with the simplified format, there are other complications. There may be such challenges as playing in various keys (lots of black notes), various time signatures, and difficult rhythms.

How *Your First Fake Book* Makes Playing Easier

We have taken special care to make this book as easy to use as possible. Melodies have been simplified, the number of chords needed has been reduced to a minimum, and rhythms have been reduced to what anyone with a few months of study will know. The print is large, and the songs are laid out to emphasize their simplicity. Where the melody repeats with different words, that is made obvious as well.

The Key of C: Keeping Black Notes to a Minimum

If you have had any classical music study, you may be aware that when a collection of sharps or flats appears at the left of every line, that tells you that the piece is in a certain key. Practically, that means that every time you encounter those notes, they are automatically played as sharps or flats. In this book, you will not have to be concerned with any of that, as all the songs are arranged in the key of C.

A Few Chords to Play Many Songs

Unlike professionally oriented fakebooks, where you will find many different chords, and some of those quite difficult, most of the songs in this book can be played with a dozen or so chords. In fact, many of the songs can be played with only two or three chords. All the chords chosen for this volume are easy to play and fit naturally under the hand.

Finally, the songs have been chosen to represent a variety of styles, including many of the best-loved and most requested standards. I hope this collection helps start you on the path of creativity and comfortable music making. Using melody and chords is one of the best ways to understand the structure of all music and will lead you nicely to further study in classical, jazz, rock and any other type of music you like. Enjoy the journey!

Alexander Citron

AIN'T MISBEHAVIN'
from AIN'T MISBEHAVIN'

Words by ANDY RAZAF
Music by THOMAS WALLER and HARRY BROOKS

ALEXANDER'S RAGTIME BAND

Words and Music by
IRVING BERLIN

Come on and hear,   come on and hear   Al - ex -

an - der's Rag - time Band.   Come on and hear,   come on and

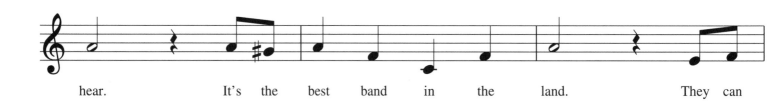

hear.   It's the best band in the land.   They can

play a bu - gle call like you nev - er heard be - fore,   so nat - u - ral that you

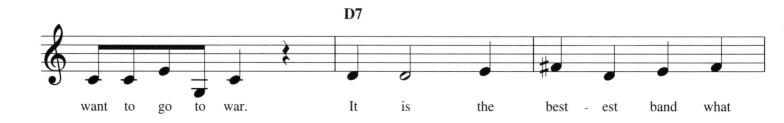

want to go to war.   It is the best - est band what

am, hon - ey lamb. Come on a - long, come on a -

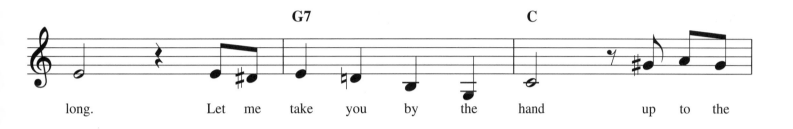

long. Let me take you by the hand up to the

man, up to the man who's the lead - er of the

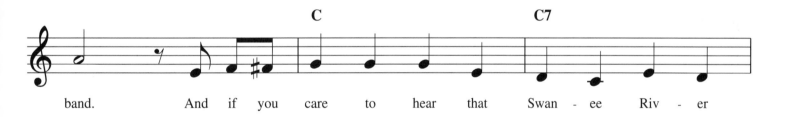

band. And if you care to hear that Swan - ee Riv - er

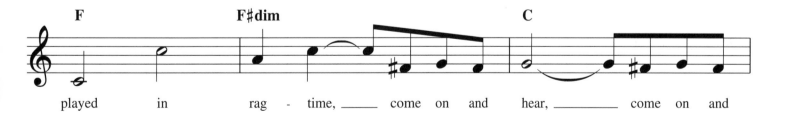

played in rag - time, _____ come on and hear, _____ come on and

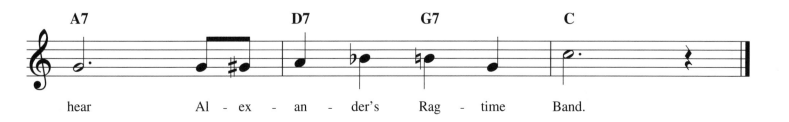

hear Al - ex - an - der's Rag - time Band.

ALL THE THINGS YOU ARE

from VERY WARM FOR MAY

Lyrics by OSCAR HAMMERSTEIN II
Music by JEROME KERN

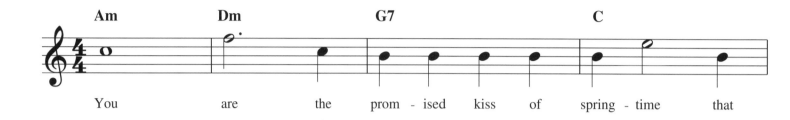

You are the prom - ised kiss of spring - time that

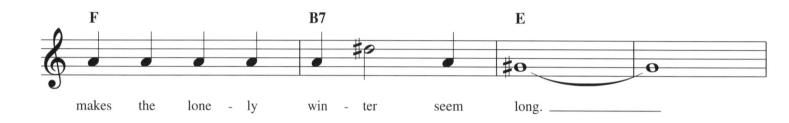

makes the lone - ly win - ter seem long. _____

You are the breath - less hush of eve - ning that

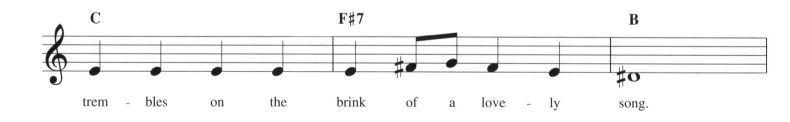

trem - bles on the brink of a love - ly song.

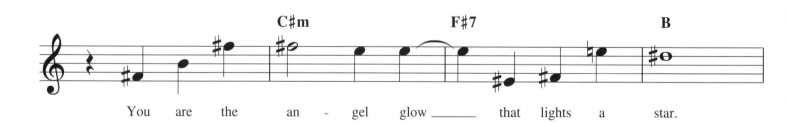

You are the an - gel glow _____ that lights a star.

The dear - est things I know ____ are what you are. _____

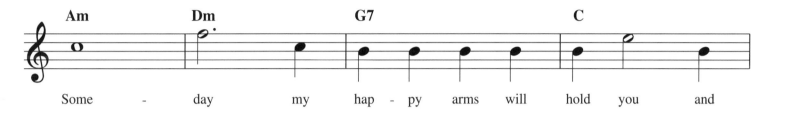

Some - day my hap - py arms will hold you and

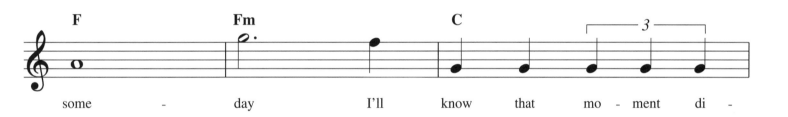

some - day I'll know that mo - ment di -

vine, when all the things you are are mine.

ALLEY CAT SONG

Words by JACK HARLEN
Music by FRANK BJORN

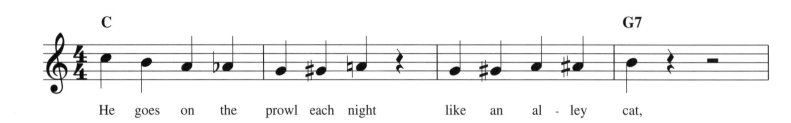

He goes on the prowl each night like an al - ley cat,

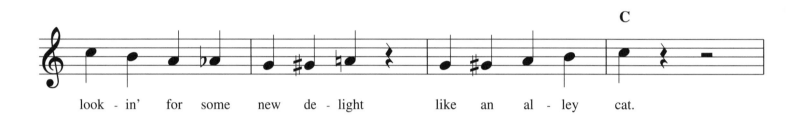

look - in' for some new de - light like an al - ley cat.

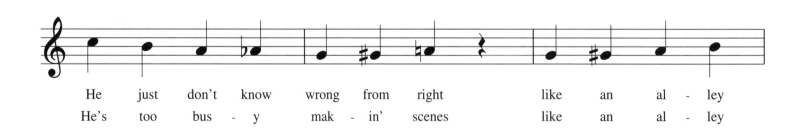

She can't trust him out of sight, there's no doubt of that.
He don't know what "faith - ful" means, there's no doubt of that.

He just don't know wrong from right like an al - ley
He's too bus - y mak - in' scenes like an al - ley

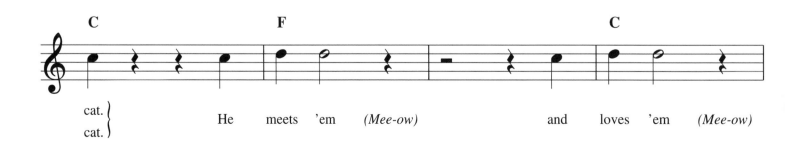

cat.
cat. He meets 'em (Mee-ow) and loves 'em (Mee-ow)

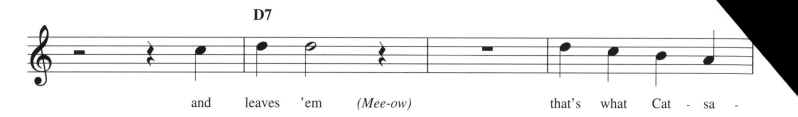

D7

and   leaves   'em   *(Mee-ow)*   that's   what   Cat -   sa -

G7   **C**

no - va   does.   It's   no   way   to   treat   a   pal,   she   should   tell   him,

G7

"Scat!"   Aren't   you   sor - ry   for   that   gal

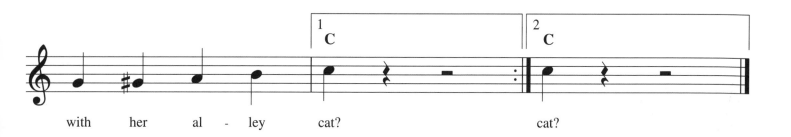

1 **C**   **2** **C**

with   her   al - ley   cat?   cat?

AMERICA THE BEAUTIFUL

Words by KATHERINE LEE BATES
Music by SAMUEL A. WARD

*Asterisks show chords which may be left out by beginning students

AS LONG AS HE NEEDS ME

from the Columbia Pictures - Romulus film OLIVER!

Words and Music by
LIONEL BART

ANNIE'S SONG

Music Publishing Company, Inc. (ASCAP)
...AP)
...amWorks Songs Administered by
...sic Publishing Company, Inc.
...al Copyright Secured   All Rights Reserved

Words and Music by
JOHN DENVER

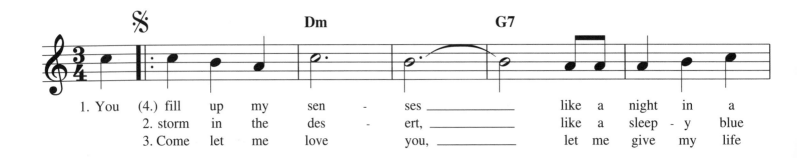

1. You   (4.) fill   up   my   sen - ses _____   like   a   night   in   a
2. storm   in   the   des - ert, _____   like   a   sleep - y   blue
3. Come   let   me   love   you, _____   let   me   give   my   life

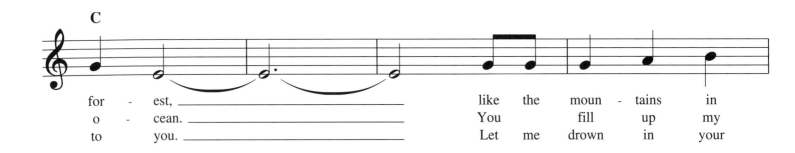

for - est, _____   like   the   moun - tains   in
o - cean. _____   You   fill   up   my
to   you. _____   Let   me   drown   in   your

spring - time, _____   like   a   walk   in   the   rain. _____
sens - es, _____
laugh - ter, _____

____   Like   a   ____   come   fill   me   a - gain. _____

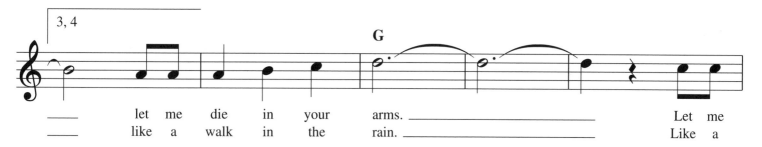

3, 4

G

_____ let me die in your arms. _____ Let me
_____ like a walk in the rain. _____ Like a

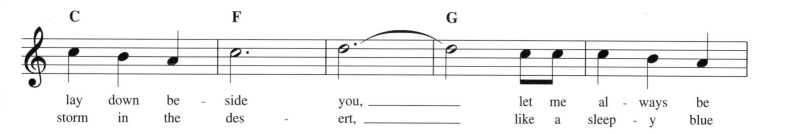

C   **F**   **G**

lay down be - side you, _____ let me al - ways be
storm in the des - ert, _____ like a sleep - y blue

C   **Dm**   **Em**

with you. _____ Come let me love you, _____
o - cean. _____ You fill up my sens - es, _____

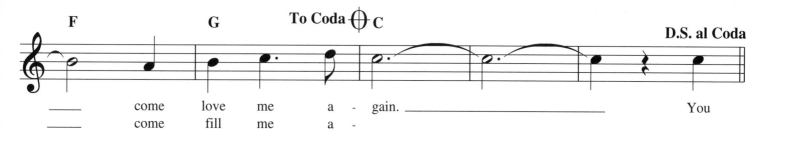

F   **G**   **To Coda** ⊕ **C**   **D.S. al Coda**

_____ come love me a - gain. _____ You
_____ come fill me a -

CODA

⊕

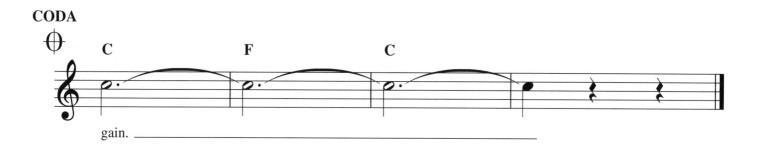

C   **F**   **C**

gain. _____

BEAUTY AND THE BEAST
from Walt Disney's BEAUTY AND THE BEAST

Words by HOWARD ASHMAN
Music by ALAN MENKEN

BLAME IT ON MY YOUTH

Words by EDWARD HEY...
Music by OSCAR LEVA...

BEWITCHED
from PAL JOEY

Words by LORENZ HART
Music by RICHARD RODGERS

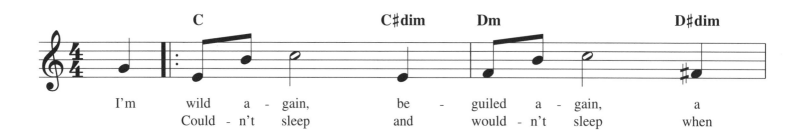

I'm wild a - gain, be - guiled a - gain, a
Could - n't sleep and would - n't sleep when

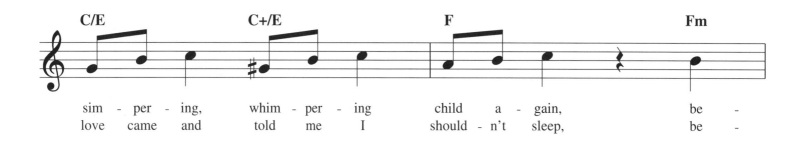

sim - per - ing, whim - per - ing child a - gain, be -
love came and told me I should - n't sleep, be -

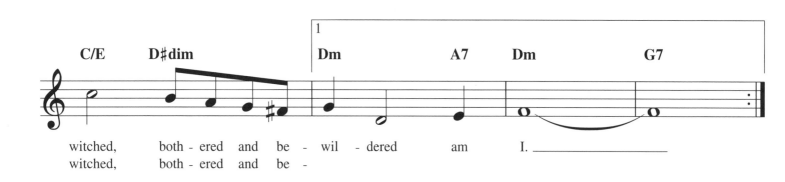

witched, both - ered and be - wil - dered am I. _____
witched, both - ered and be -

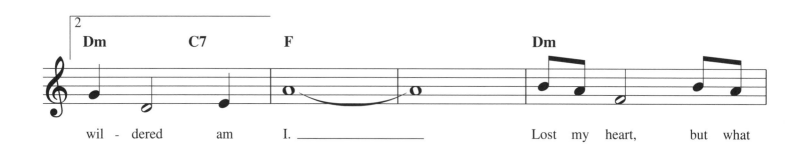

wil - dered am I. _____ Lost my heart, but what

of it. He is cold, I a - gree.

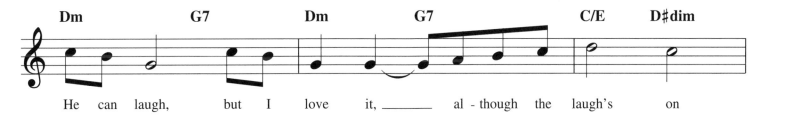

He can laugh, but I love it, _____ al - though the laugh's on

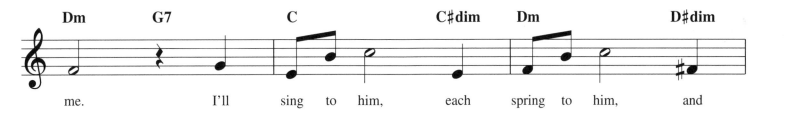

me. I'll sing to him, each spring to him, and

long for the day when I'll cling to him, be -

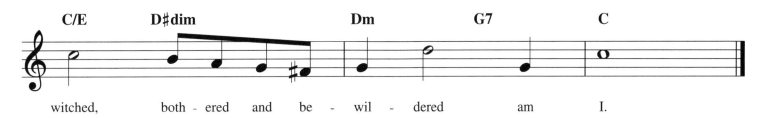

witched, both - ered and be - wil - dered am I.

BLUE AND SENTIMENTAL

Words and Music by MACK DAVID,
JERRY LIVINGSTON and COUNT BASIE

BLUE SUEDE SHOES

Words and M
CARL LEE PER

Well it's one for the mon - ey, two for the show,

three to get read - y now go, cat, go but don't you

step on my blue suede shoes. You can

do an - y - thing___ but lay off of my blue suede shoes. ___

___ Well you can knock me down, __ step on my face, __

slan - der my name all o - ver the place.__ Do an - y - thing that you

want to do but uh - uh hon - ey, lay off of my shoes. __

Don't you step on my blue suede shoes. ___

BLUEBERRY HILL

Words and Music by AL LEWIS,
LARRY STOCK and VINCENT ROSE

CAN YOU FEEL THE LOVE TONIGHT
from Walt Disney Pictures' THE LION KING

Music by ELTON JOHN
Lyrics by TIM RICE

BRING HIM HOME
from LES MISÉRABLES

Music by CLAUDE-MICHEL SCHÖNBERG
Lyrics by HERBERT KRETZMER and ALAIN BOUBLIL

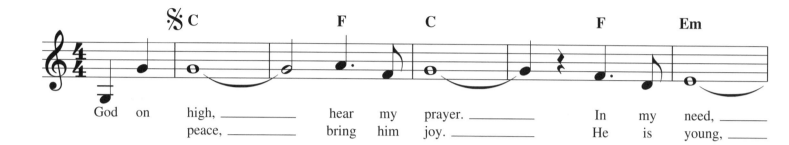

God on high, _____ hear my prayer. _____ In my need, _____
peace, _____ bring him joy. _____ He is young, _____

_____ you have al-ways been there. _____ He is young, _____
_____ he is on-ly a boy. _____ You can take, _____

_____ he's a-fraid. Let him rest, _____ heav-en blessed.
_____ you can give. Let him be, _____ let him live.

Bring him home, _____ bring him home, _____ bring him home.
If I die, _____ let me die, _____ let him

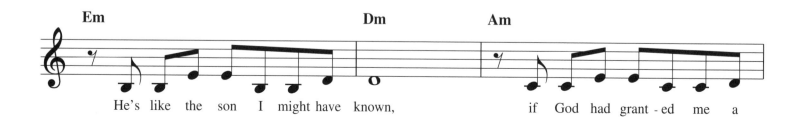

He's like the son I might have known, if God had grant-ed me a

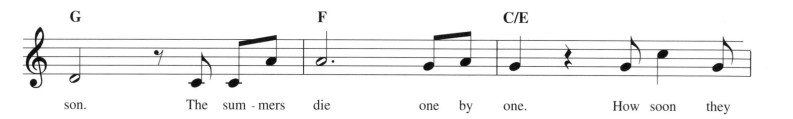

son. The sum - mers die one by one. How soon they

fly on and on. And I am old _____ and will be

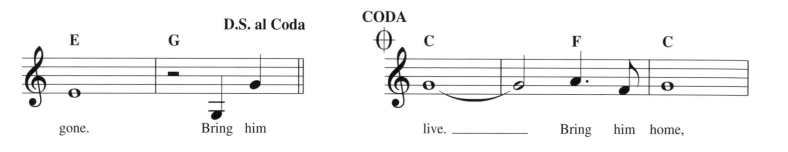

gone. Bring him live. _____ Bring him home,

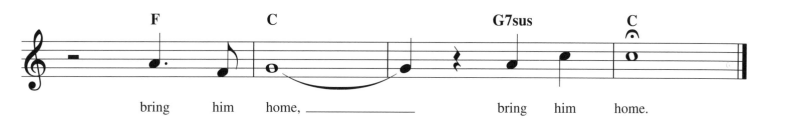

bring him home, _____ bring him home.

BYE BYE LOVE

Words and Music by FELICE BRYANT
and BOUDLEAUX BRYANT

OF BRYANT PUBLICATIONS, Gatlinburg, TN

ACUFF-ROSE-OPRYLAND MUSIC, INC., Nashville, TN

25

There goes my ba - by _____ with some - one new.

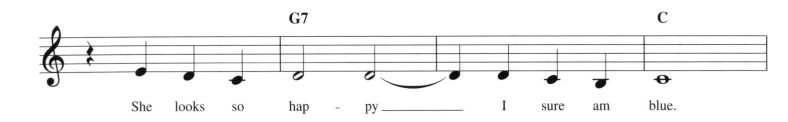

She looks so hap - py _____ I sure am blue.

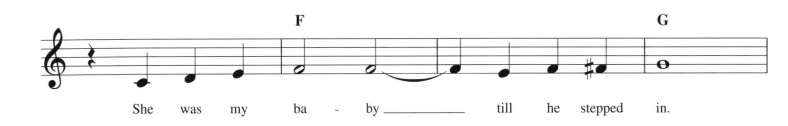

She was my ba - by _____ till he stepped in.

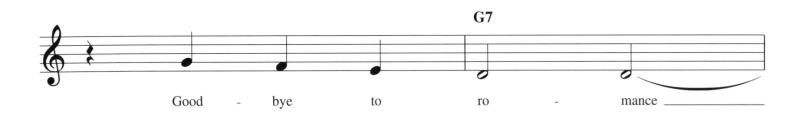

Good - bye to ro - mance _____

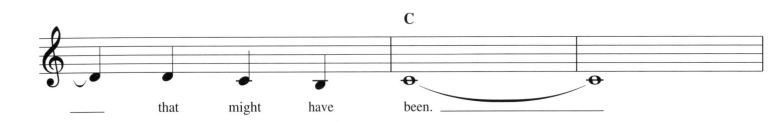

___ that might have been. _____

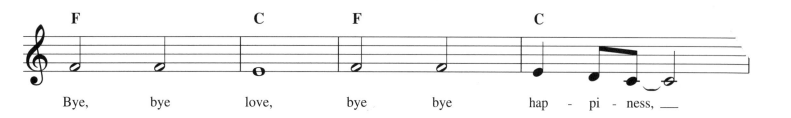

Bye, bye love, bye bye hap - pi - ness, ___

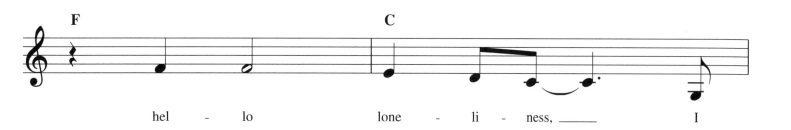

hel - lo lone - li - ness, ___ I

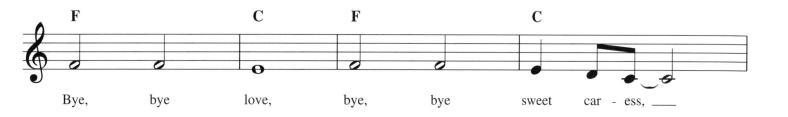

think I'm gon - na cry. ___

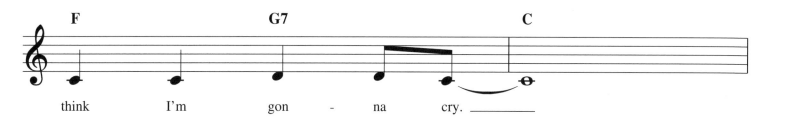

Bye, bye love, bye, bye sweet car - ess, ___

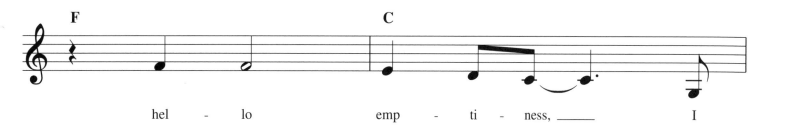

hel - lo emp - ti - ness, ___ I

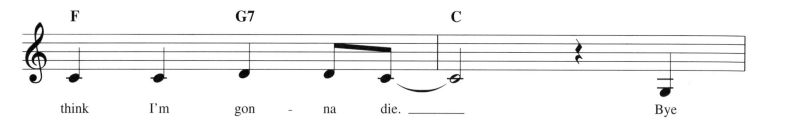

think I'm gon - na die. ___ Bye

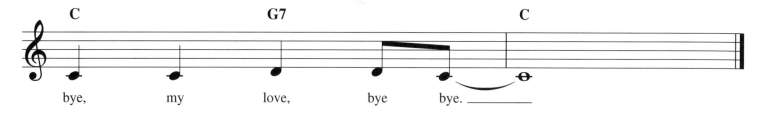

bye, my love, bye bye. ___

CAN'T HELP FALLING IN LOVE
from BLUE HAWAII

Words and Music by GEORGE DAVID WEISS,
HUGO PERETTI and LUIGI CREATORE

Wise   men   say   on - ly   fools   rush   in.   But
Shall   I   stay?   Would   it   be   a   sin?   If

I   can't   help   fall - ing   in   love   with   you.

Like   a   riv - er   flows   sure - ly   to   the   sea,

dar - ling,   so   it   goes,   some   things ___   are   meant   to   be.

Take   my   hand,   take   my   whole   life   too.   For

I   can't   help   fall - ing   in   love   with   you.   For

I   can't   help   fall - ing   in   love   with   you.

CHARIOTS OF FIRE

Music by VANGELIS

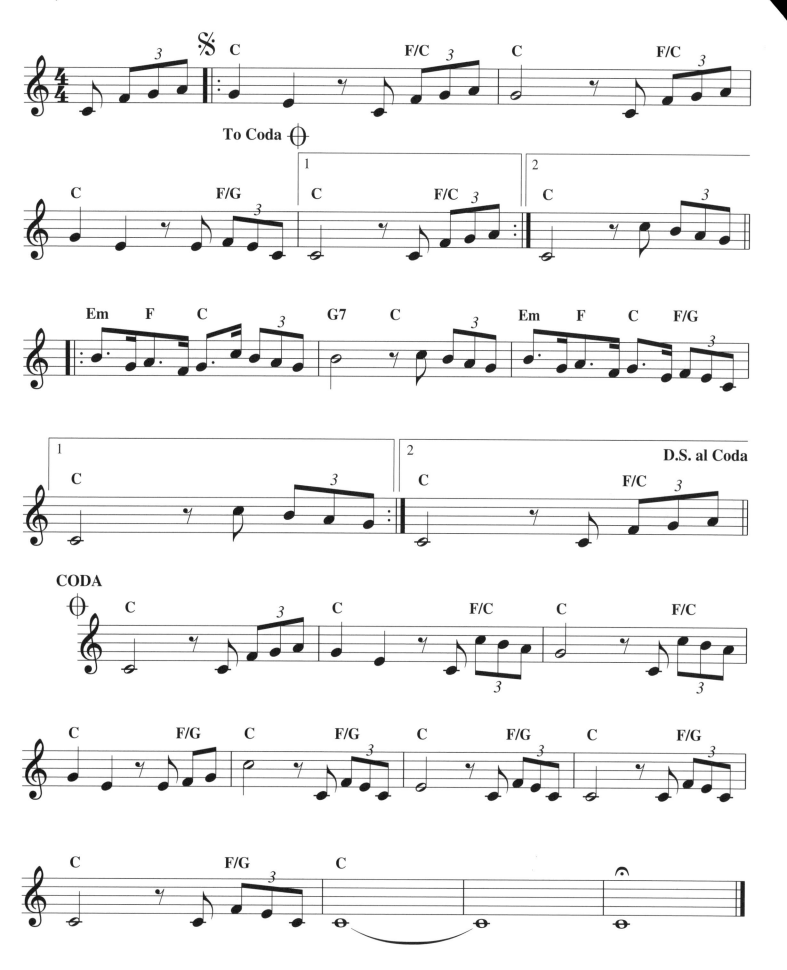

CAN'T HELP LOVIN' DAT MAN

from SHOW BOAT

Lyrics by OSCAR HAMMERSTEIN II
Music by JEROME KERN

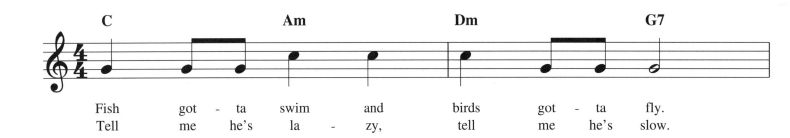

Fish got - ta swim and birds got - ta fly.
Tell me he's la - zy, tell me he's slow.

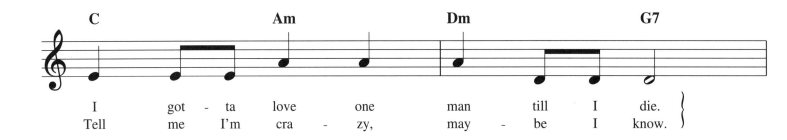

I got - ta love one man till I die.
Tell me I'm cra - zy, may - be I know.

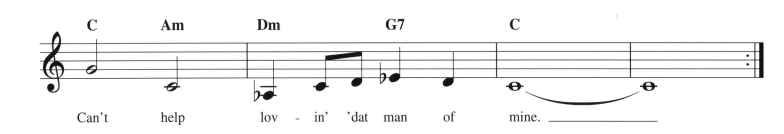

Can't help lov - in' 'dat man of mine. _____

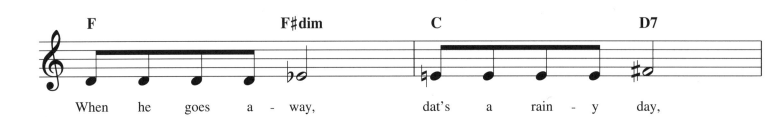

When he goes a - way, dat's a rain - y day,

and when he comes back dat day is fine. _____ 'De sun will

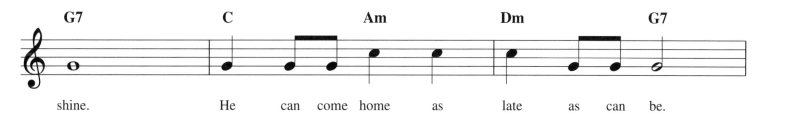

shine. He can come home as late as can be.

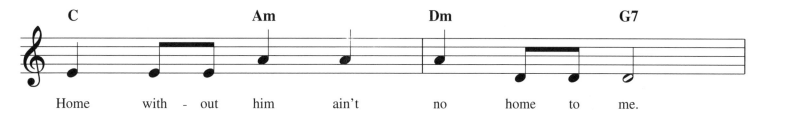

Home with - out him ain't no home to me.

Can't help lov - in' 'dat man of mine. _____

CAN'T SMILE WITHOUT YOU

Words and Music by CHRIS ARNOLD,
DAVID MARTIN and GEOFF MORROW

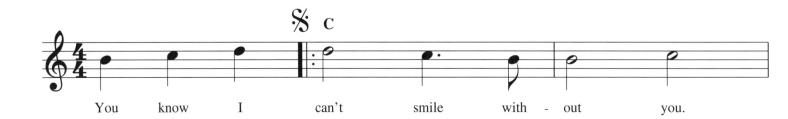

You know I can't smile with - out you.

I can't smile with - out you. I can't laugh and I

can't sing. I'm find-ing it hard __ to do an-y-thing. __ You see, I

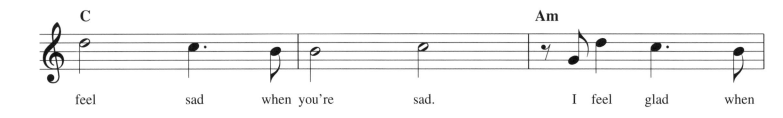

feel sad when you're sad. I feel glad when

you're glad. If you on-ly knew what I'm go-ing through.

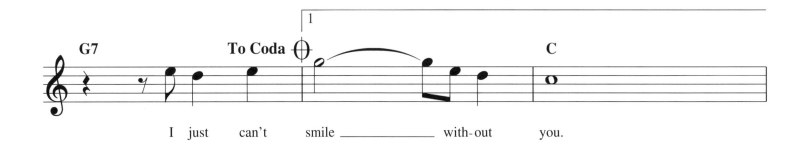

I just can't smile _____ with-out you.

You came a - long ___ just like a song ___ and

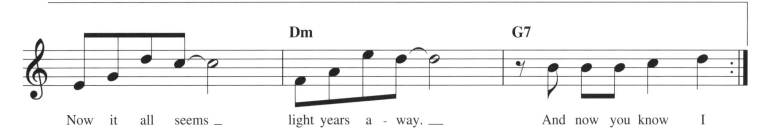

Dm   **G7**   **C**

bright-ened my day. ___ Who'd have be-lieved that you were part of a dream. ___

Dm   **G7**

Now it all seems ___ light years a - way. ___ And now you know I

2   **G7**   **Gm**

smile. Now some peo - ple say ___ hap - pi - ness takes ___

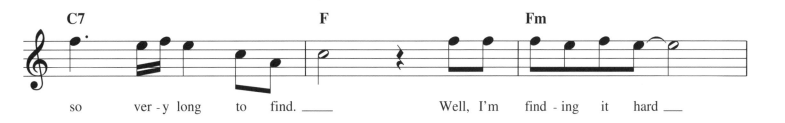

C7   **F**   **Fm**

so ver - y long to find. ___ Well, I'm find - ing it hard ___

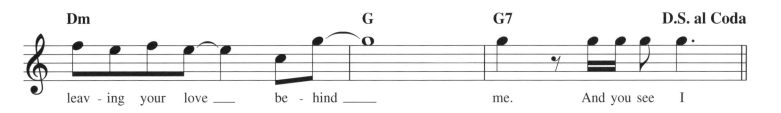

Dm   **G**   **G7**   **D.S. al Coda**

leav - ing your love ___ be - hind ___ me. And you see I

CODA

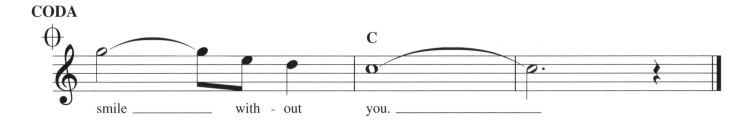

                                    C

smile ___ with - out you. ___

CAROLINA IN THE MORNING

Lyrics by GUS KAHN
Music by WALTER DONALDSON

Noth-ing could be fi - ner than to be in Car - o - li - na in the morn -
Stroll-ing with my girl - ie where the dew is pearl - y ear - ly in the morn -

ing. Noth-ing could be sweet - er than my sweet-heart when I meet her in the
ing, but - ter - flies all flut - ter up and kiss each lit - tle but - ter - cup at

morn - ing. When the morn - ing
dawn - ing.

glo - ries twine a - round the door.

whis - per - ing pret - ty sto - ries I long to hear once

more. If I had A - lad - din's lamp for on - ly a day, ___

I'd make a wish and here's what I'd say, ___ noth - ing could be fi - ner than to

be in Car - o - li - na in the morn - ing.

COMEDY TONIGHT

from A FUNNY THING HAPPENED ON THE WAY TO THE FORUM

Words and Music by
STEPHEN SONDHEIM

Some - thing fa - mil - iar, some - thing pe - cul - iar,
Some - thing ap - peal - ing, some - thing ap - pal - ling,

some - thing for ev - 'ry - one, a com - e - dy to - night.
some - thing for ev - 'ry - one, a com - e - dy to - night.

Noth - ing with kings, noth - ing with crowns.

Bring on the lov - ers, li - ars and clowns! _____

Old sit - u - a - tions, new com - pli - ca - tions,

noth - ing por - ten - tous or po - lite. _____

Tra - ge - dy to - mor - row, com - e - dy to - night.

COLORS OF THE WIND
from Walt Disney's POCAHONTAS

Music by ALAN MENKEN
Lyrics by STEPHEN SCHWARTZ

CODA

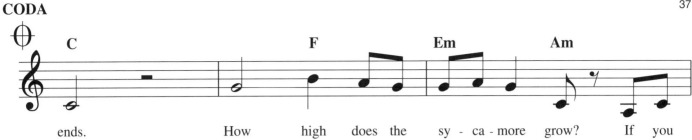

ends.   How high does the sy - ca - more grow?   If you

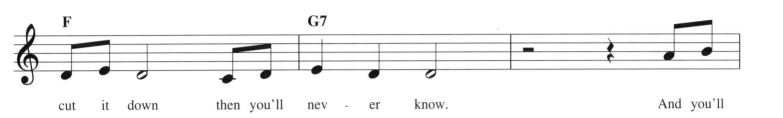

cut it down   then you'll nev - er know.   And you'll

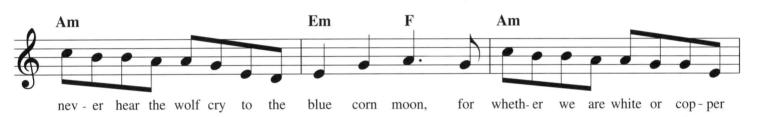

nev - er hear the wolf cry to the blue corn moon,   for wheth- er we are white or cop - per

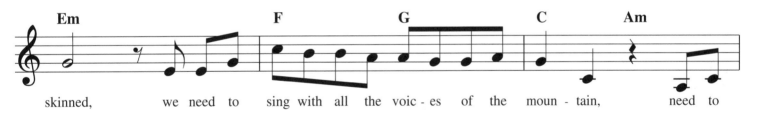

skinned,   we need to sing with all the voic - es of the moun - tain,   need to

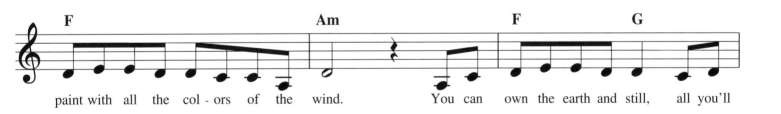

paint with all the col - ors of the wind.   You can own the earth and still, all you'll

own is earth un - til you can paint with all the col - ors of the wind.

DINAH
from THE BIG BROADCAST

Words by SAM M. LEWIS and JOE YOUNG
Music by HARRY AKST

DO-RE-MI
from THE SOUND OF MUSIC

Lyrics by OSCAR HAMMERSTEIN
Music by RICHARD RODGERS

DON'T GET AROUND MUCH ANYMORE

Words and Music by BOB RUSSELL
and DUKE ELLINGTON

Missed the Sat - ur - day dance, _____ heard they crowd - ed the floor. _____
got as far as the door. _

Could - n't bear it with - out you,
They'd have asked me a - bout you,

don't get a - round much an - y - more. Thought I'd vis - it the club, _

more. Dar - ling I guess my

mind's more at ease. But nev - er - the -

less, why stir up mem - o - ries? Been in - vit - ed on dates, _____

might have gone but what for? _____ Aw - f'lly dif - f'rent with -

out you, don't get a - round much an - y - more. _____

DON'T CRY FOR ME ARGENTINA

from EVITA

Words by TIM RICE
Music by ANDREW LLOYD WEBBER

MCA music publishing

It won't be ea - sy. You'll think it

strange when I try to ex - plain how I feel, that I

still need your love af - ter all that I've done. You won't be -

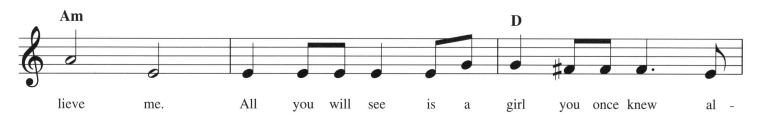

lieve me. All you will see is a girl you once knew al -

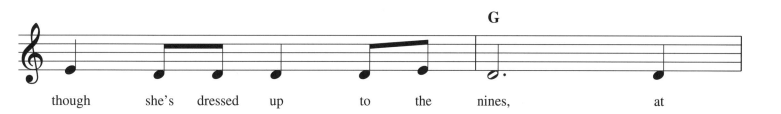

though she's dressed up to the nines, at

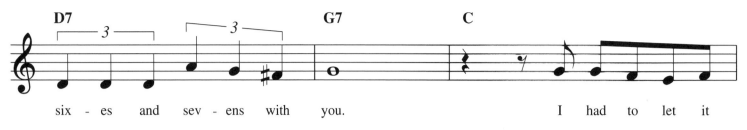

six - es and sev - ens with you. I had to let it

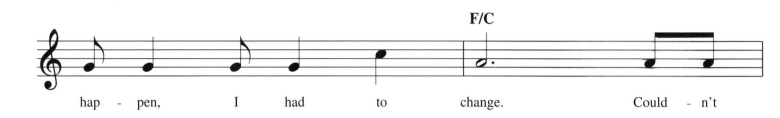

hap - pen, I had to change. Could - n't

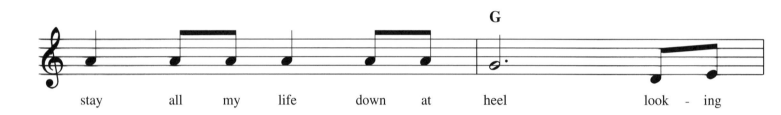

stay all my life down at heel look - ing

out of the win - dow, stay - ing out of the sun.

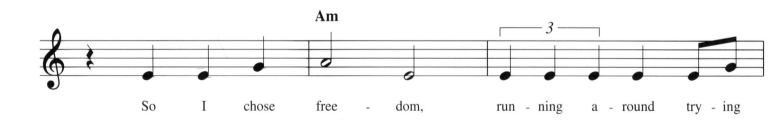

So I chose free - dom, run - ning a - round try - ing

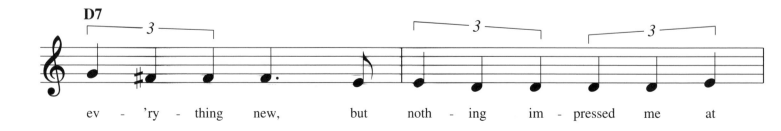

ev - 'ry - thing new, but noth - ing im - pressed me at

DON'T KNOW MUCH

Words and Music by BARRY MANN,
CYNTHIA WEIL and TOM SNOW

Look at this face,   I know the years are show - ing.
Look at these eyes,   they've nev - er seen what mat - ters.
Look at this man,   so blessed with in - spi - ra - tion.

Look at this life,   I still don't know where _ it's go - ing.
Look at these dreams,   so beat - en and _ so bat - tered.
Look at this soul,   still search-ing for ___ sal - va - tion.

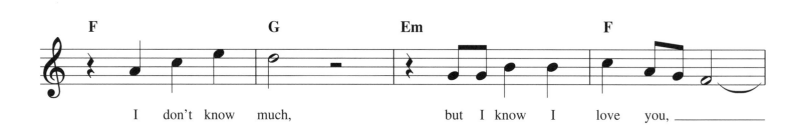

I don't know much,   but I know I love you, _____

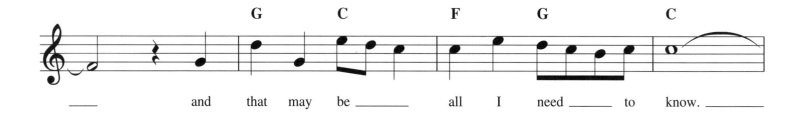

____ and that may be _____ all I need _____ to know. _____

45

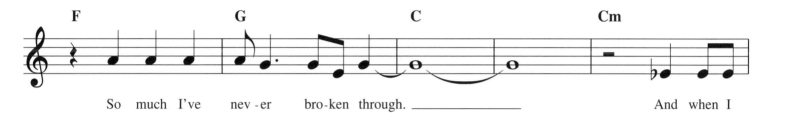

So man-y ques-tions still left un - an-swered.

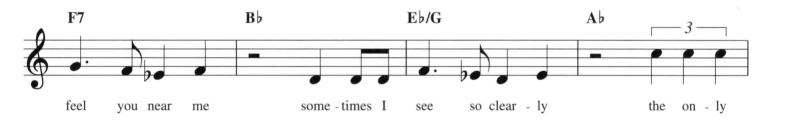

So much I've nev-er bro-ken through. _____ And when I

feel you near me some-times I see so clear-ly the on-ly

truth I've ev-er known is me and you. _____

EARTH ANGEL

Words and Music by
JESSE BELVIN

Earth An - gel, Earth An - gel, will you be mine, __ my dar - ling dear, __

love me all the time. __ I'm just a fool, __ a fool in love with

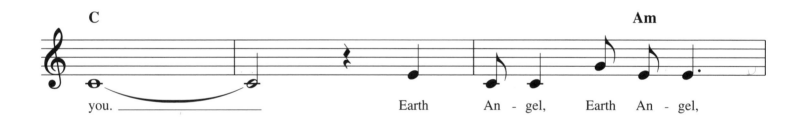

you. __ Earth An - gel, Earth An - gel,

the one I a - dore, _____ love you for - ev - er and ev - er - more. __

I'm just a fool, __ a fool in love with you. _____ I

fell for you, ___ and I knew the vi - sion of your love's love - li -

ness. _____ I hope and I pray ___ that some - day ___ I'll be the

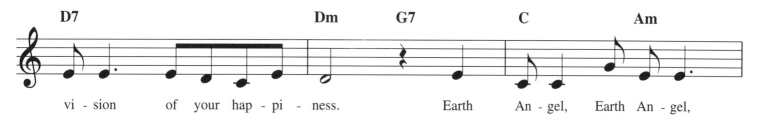

vi - sion of your hap - pi - ness. Earth An - gel, Earth An - gel,

please be mine, __ my dar - ling dear, __ love you all the time. __

I'm just a fool, __ a fool in love with you. _____

EDELWEISS
from THE SOUND OF MUSIC

...nd Oscar Hammerstein II
...ion and allied rights throughout the world
...hts Reserved

Lyrics by OSCAR HAMMERSTEIN II
Music by RICHARD RODGERS

FASCINATION

Words by DICK MANNING
Music by F.D. MARCHETTI

EV'RY TIME WE SAY GOODBYE

from SEVEN LIVELY ARTS

Words and Music by
COLE PORTER

Ev - 'ry time _____ we say good - bye I die _____ a lit - tle.

Ev - 'ry time _____ we say good - bye _____ I won - der

why _____ a lit - tle. Why the gods a - bove me who

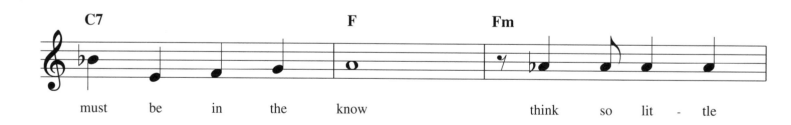

must be in the know think so lit - tle

of me they al - low you to go. _____

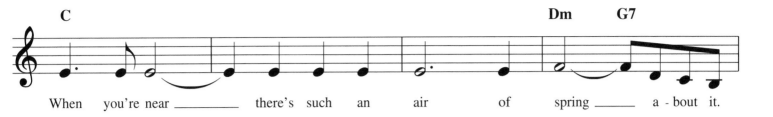

C   **Dm**   **G7**

When you're near _____ there's such an air of spring _____ a - bout it.

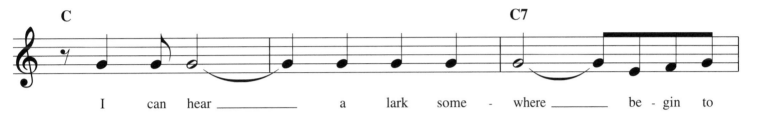

C   **C7**

I can hear _____ a lark some - where _____ be - gin to

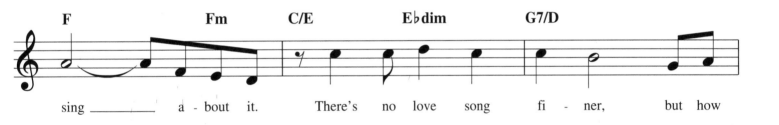

F   **Fm**   **C/E**   **E♭dim**   **G7/D**

sing _____ a - bout it. There's no love song fi - ner, but how

C7   **F**   **Fm**   **C/G**   **Am**

strange the change from ma - jor to mi - nor ev - 'ry time _____

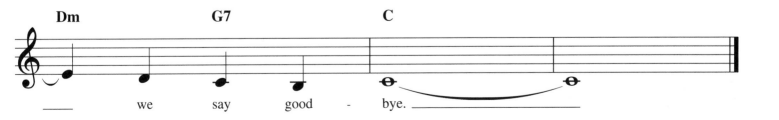

Dm   **G7**   **C**

____ we say good - bye. _____

FALLING IN LOVE WITH LOVE
from THE BOYS FROM SYRACUSE

Words by LORENZ HART
Music by RICHARD RODGERS

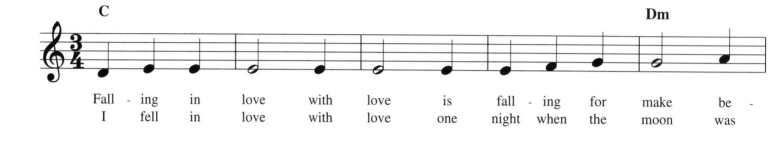

Fall - ing   in   love   with   love   is   fall - ing   for   make   be -
I   fell   in   love   with   love   one   night   when   the   moon   was

lieve. _____
full. _____

Fall - ing   in   love   with
I   was   un - wise   with

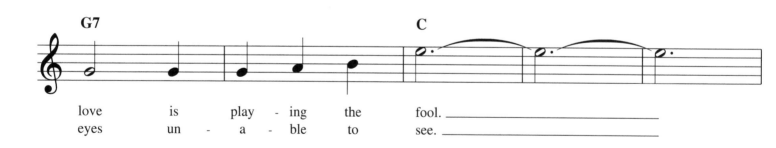

love   is   play - ing   the   fool. _____
eyes   un - a - ble   to   see. _____

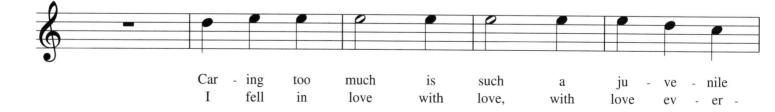

Car - ing   too   much   is   such   a   ju - ve - nile
I   fell   in   love   with   love,   with   love   ev - er -

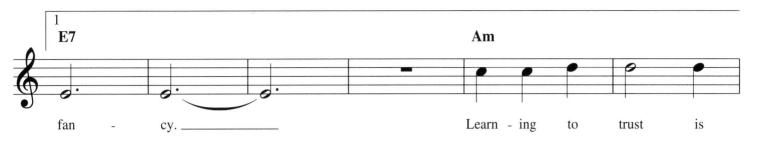

1   **E7**   **Am**

fan - cy. _____ Learn - ing to trust is

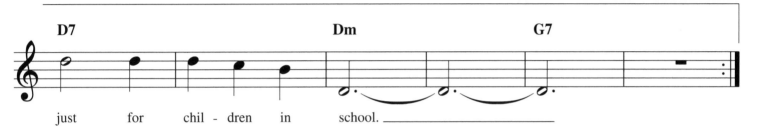

D7   **Dm**   **G7**

just for chil - dren in school. _____

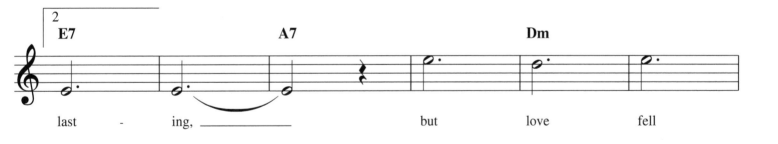

2   **E7**   **A7**   **Dm**

last - ing, _____ but love fell

G7   **C**

out with me. _____

GEORGIA ON MY MIND

Words by STUART GORRELL
Music by HOAGY CARMICHAEL

GOODNIGHT, IRENE

Words and Music by HUDDIE LE
and JOHN . LOMAX

GET ME TO THE CHURCH ON TIME

from MY FAIR LADY

Words by ALAN JAY LERNER
Music by FREDERICK LOEWE

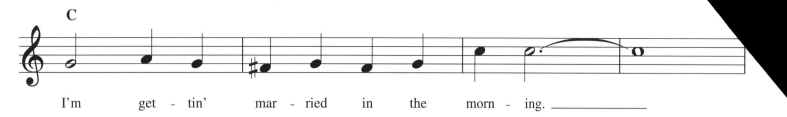

C

I'm get - tin' mar - ried in the morn - ing. _____

Ding! Dong! The bells are gon - na chime. _____

F   F#dim   C/G   A7

Kick up a rum - pus, but don't lose the com - pass; and

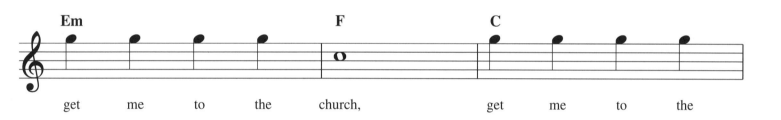

Em   F   C

get me to the church, get me to the

D7   C/G

church, for Pete's sake get me to the

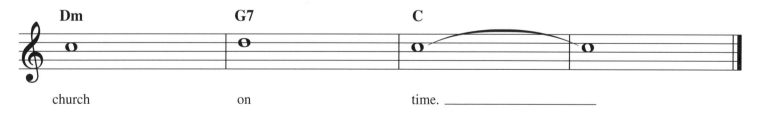

Dm   G7   C

church on time. _____

GETTING TO KNOW YOU

from THE KING AND I

l Rodgers and Oscar Hammerstein II

of publication and allied rights throughout the world
ed   All Rights Reserved

Lyrics by OSCAR HAMMERSTEIN II
Music by RICHARD RODGERS

Get - ting to know you, get - ting to know all a -

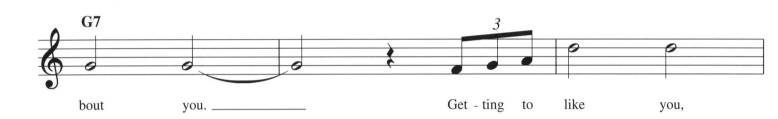

bout you. _____ Get - ting to like you,

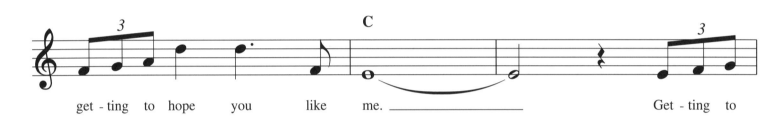

get - ting to hope you like me. _____ Get - ting to

know you, put - ting it my way but nice - ly, _____

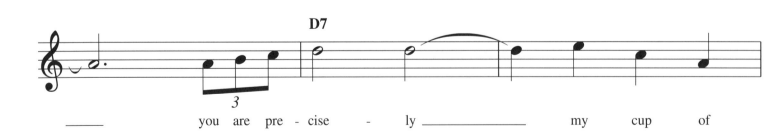

___ you are pre - cise - ly _____ my cup of

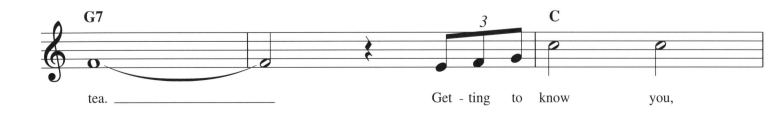

tea. _____ Get - ting to know you,

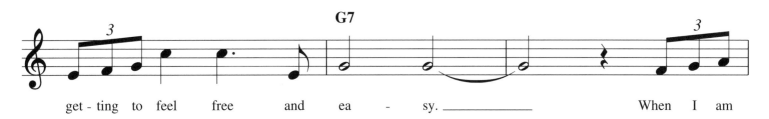

get - ting to feel free and ea - sy. _____ When I am

with you, get - ting to know what to

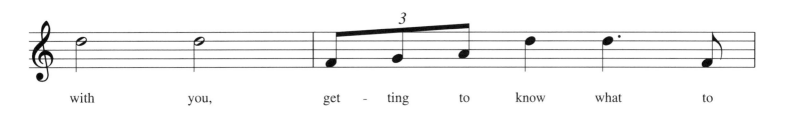

say. _____ Have - n't you no - ticed,

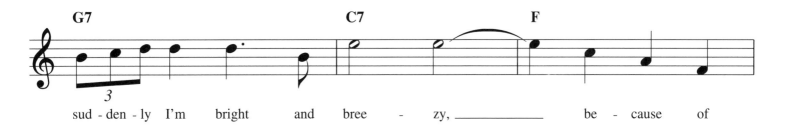

sud - den - ly I'm bright and bree - zy, _____ be - cause of

all the beau - ti - ful and new things I'm

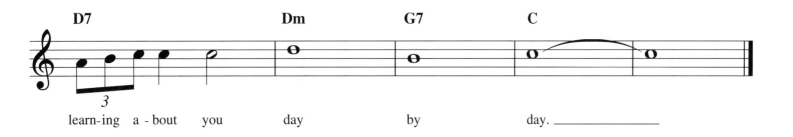

learn - ing a - bout you day by day. _____

HARBOR LIGHTS

Words and Music by JIMMY KENNEDY
and HUGH WILLIAMS

HE'S GOT THE WHOLE WORLD IN HIS HANDS

A HARD DAY'S NIGHT

Words and Music by JOHN LENNON
and PAUL McCARTNEY

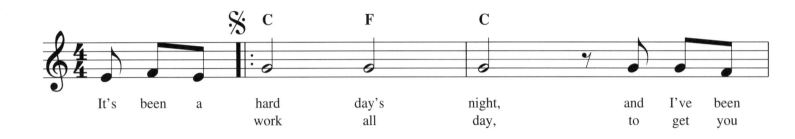

It's been a hard day's night, and I've been
work all day, to get you

work - ing _____ like a dog. _____ It's been a hard day's
mon - ey _____ to buy you things. _____ And it's ____ worth it just to hear you

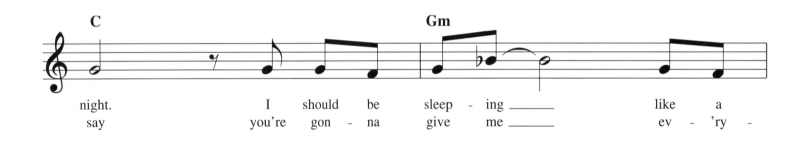

night. I should be sleep - ing _____ like a
say you're gon - na give me ____ _____ ev - 'ry -

log. _____ But when I get home to you, ____ I find the
thing. _____ So why I love to come home, ___ 'cause when I

things that you do, _____ will make me feel _____ al -
get you a - lone, _____ you know I'll be _____ O. _____

To Coda ⊕

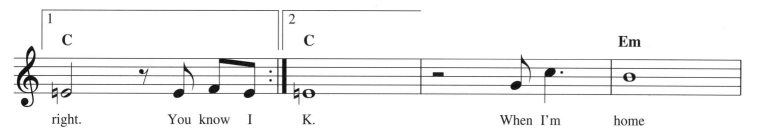

right. You know I K.   When I'm home

ev - 'ry - thing seems _ to be al - right.   When I'm home

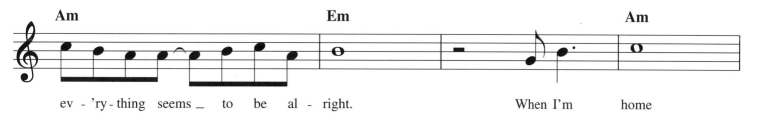

feel - ing you hold - ing me tight,   tight yeah. It's been a

CODA

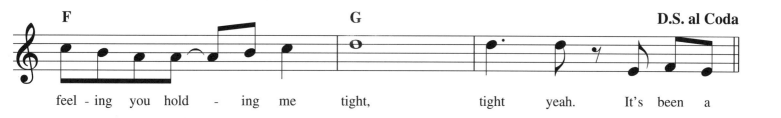

right,   you know I feel _____ al -

right,   you know I feel _____ al - right.

HEART AND SOUL
from the Paramount Short Subject A SONG IS BORN

Words by FRANK LOESSER
Music by HOAGY CARMICHAEL

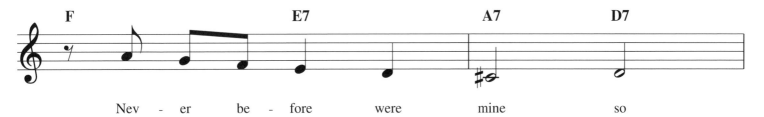

Nev - er be - fore were mine so

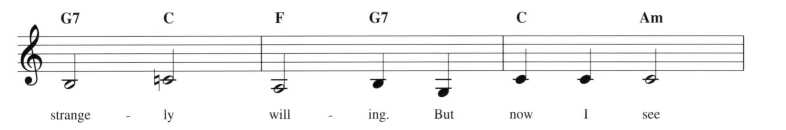

strange - ly will - ing. But now I see

what one em - brace can do. Look at me,

it's got me lov - ing you mad - ly,

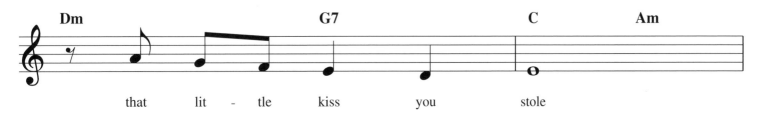

that lit - tle kiss you stole

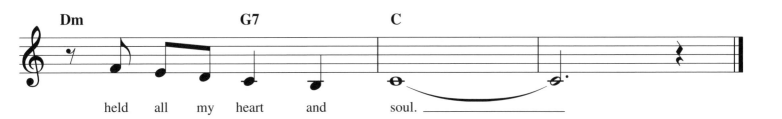

held all my heart and soul. _____

HEY JUDE

Words and Music by JOHN LENNON
and PAUL McCARTNEY

67

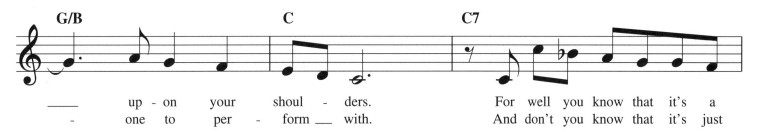

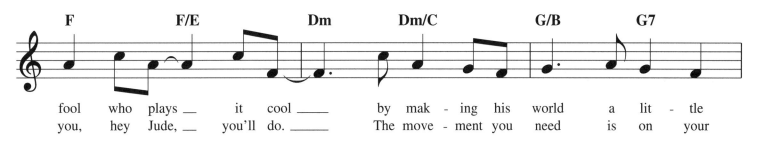

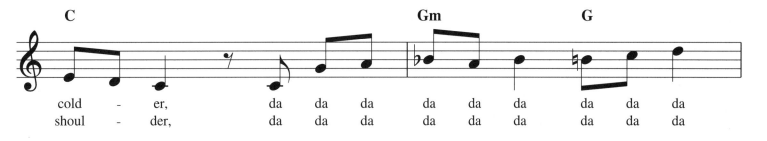

D.S. al Coda (Second time)   CODA

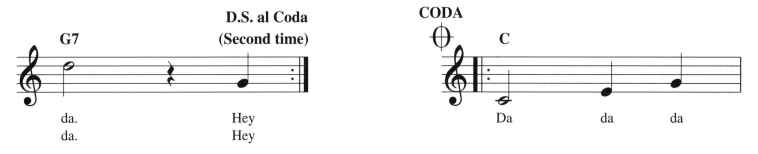

HONEYSUCKLE ROSE
from AIN'T MISBEHAVIN'

Words by ANDY RAZAF
Music by THOMAS "FATS" WALLER

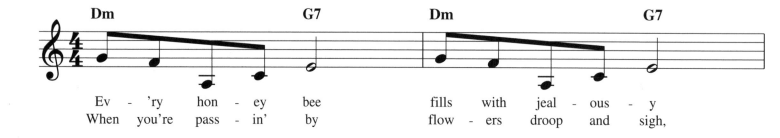

Ev - 'ry hon - ey bee fills with jeal - ous - y
When you're pass - in' by flow - ers droop and sigh,

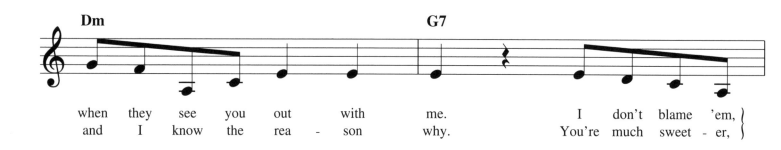

when they see you out with me.
and I know the rea - son why.

I don't blame 'em,
You're much sweet - er, }

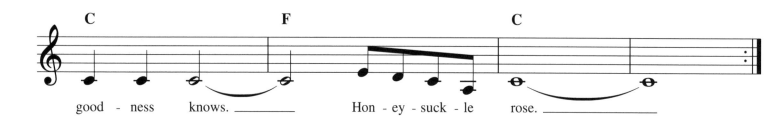

good - ness knows. _____ Hon - ey - suck - le rose. _____

Don't buy sug - ar. You just have to

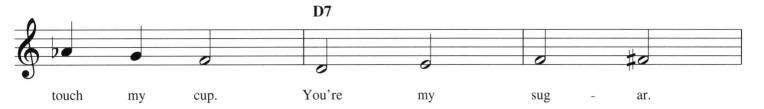

touch my cup. You're my sug - ar.

It's sweet when you stir it up. _____

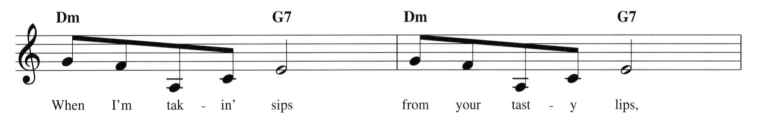

When I'm tak - in' sips from your tast - y lips,

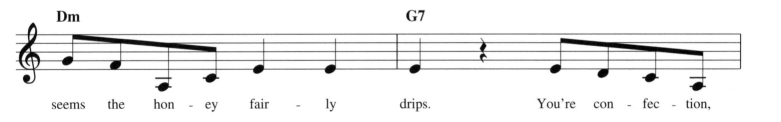

seems the hon - ey fair - ly drips. You're con - fec - tion,

good - ness knows. _____ Hon - ey - suck - le Rose. _____

HOUND DOG

Words and Music by JERRY LEIBER
and MIKE STOLLER

You ain't noth-in' but a hound dog, ___ cry-in' all the

time. You ain't noth-in' but a hound dog, ___

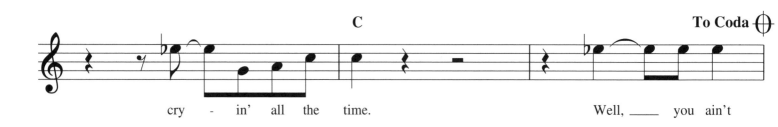

cry-in' all the time. Well, ___ you ain't

nev-er caught a rab-bit and you ain't no friend of mine. ___

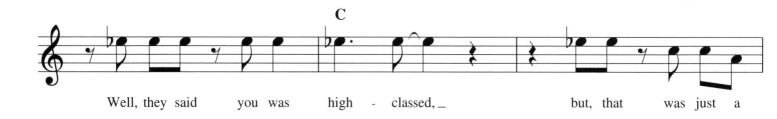

Well, they said you was high-classed, ___ but, that was just a

lie.   Yeah, they said   you was   high - classed, _

but,   that was just a lie.   Yeah, ____ you ain't

nev - er caught a rab - bit and you ain't no friend of mine. ____

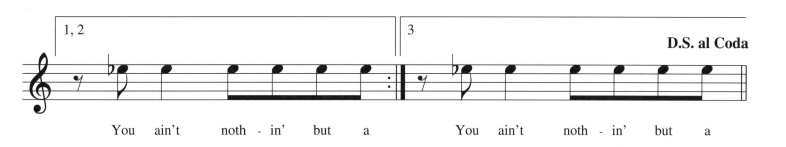

You ain't noth - in' but a   You ain't noth - in' but a

D.S. al Coda

CODA

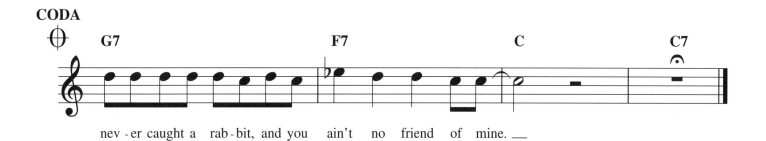

nev - er caught a rab - bit, and you ain't no friend of mine. ____

HOW SWEET IT IS
(To Be Loved by You)

Words and Music by EDWARD HOLLAND,
LAMONT DOZIER and BRIAN HOLLAND

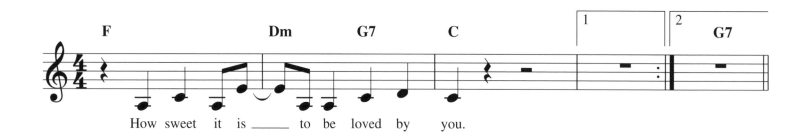

How sweet it is _____ to be loved by you.

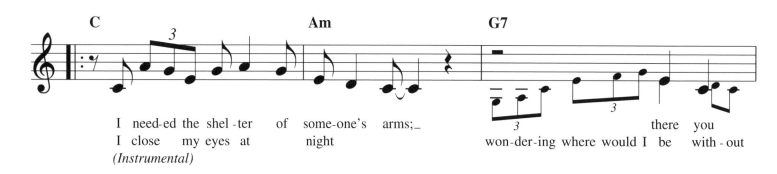

I need-ed the shel-ter of some-one's arms;_ there you
I close my eyes at night
(Instrumental)
won-der-ing where would I be with-out

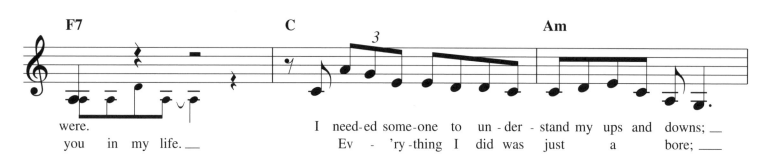

were.
you in my life._
I need-ed some-one to un-der-stand my ups and downs; _
Ev - 'ry-thing I did was just a bore; ___

there you were ___ with sweet love and de-
ev - 'ry-where I went, seems I'd been there be-fore. But you bright - en up for me
End Instrumental You were bet-ter to me than I

vo - tion deep-ly touch-ing my e - mo-tion.___
all of my days _ with a love so sweet in so man - y ways._ I want to
was to my - self; _ for me there's you and there ain't no-bod - y else. _

73

stop   and thank you, ba - by; I want __ to stop   and thank you,

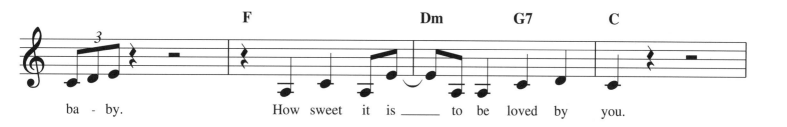

ba - by.   How sweet it is _____ to be loved by you.

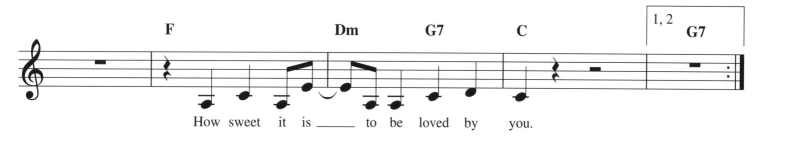

How sweet it is _____ to be loved by you.

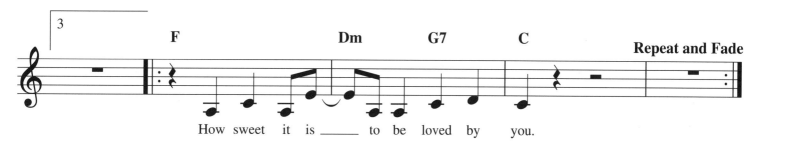

How sweet it is _____ to be loved by you.

HELLO, DOLLY!

Music and Lyric by
JERRY HERMAN

Hel - lo, Dol - ly, well hel - lo, Dol - ly. It's so nice to have you back where you be - long. You're look - ing swell, Dol - ly, I can tell, Dol - ly, you're still glow - in', you're still crow - in', you're still go - in' strong. I feel the room sway - in' for the band's play - in' one of your old fav - 'rite songs from way back when. So take her wrap, fel - las, find her an emp - ty lap, fel - las. Dol - ly - 'll nev - er go a - way a - gain.

I CAN'T GIVE YOU ANYTHING BUT LOVE

from BLACKBIRDS OF 1928

Words by DOROTHY FIELDS
Music by JIMMY McHUGH

I COULD HAVE DANCED ALL NIGHT
from MY FAIR LADY

Lerner and Frederick Loewe

publication and allied rights throughout the world
Copyright Secured   All Rights Reserved

Words by ALAN JAY LERNER
Music by FREDERICK LOEWE

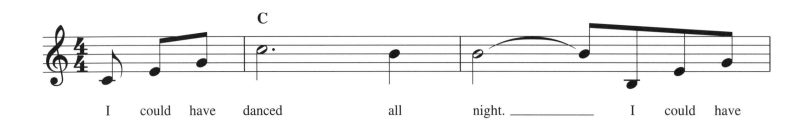

I could have danced all night._____ I could have

danced all night, and still have

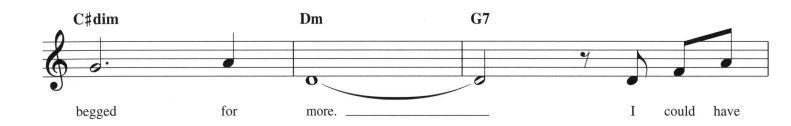

begged for more._____ I could have

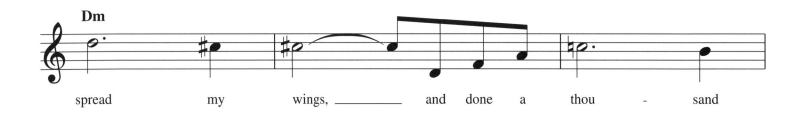

spread my wings,_____ and done a thou - sand

things I've nev - er done be -

fore._____ I'll nev - er know _____ what made it

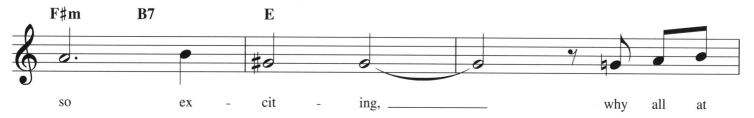

so ex - cit - ing, _____ why all at

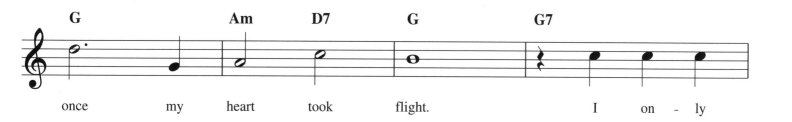

once my heart took flight. I on - ly

know, when he _____ be - gan to dance with

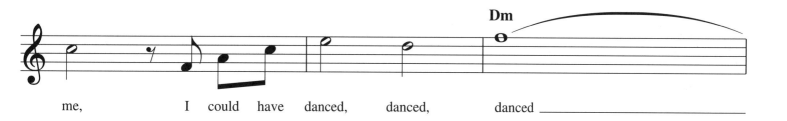

me, I could have danced, danced, danced _____

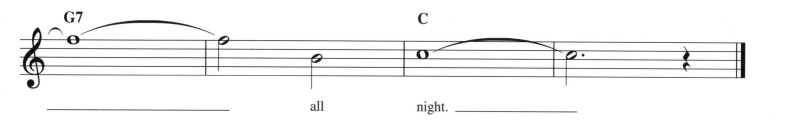

_____ all night. _____

I COULD WRITE A BOOK
from PAL JOEY

Words by LORENZ HART
Music by RICHARD RODGERS

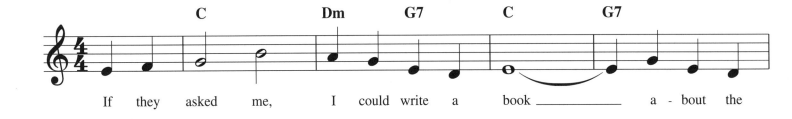

If they asked me, I could write a book _____ a - bout the

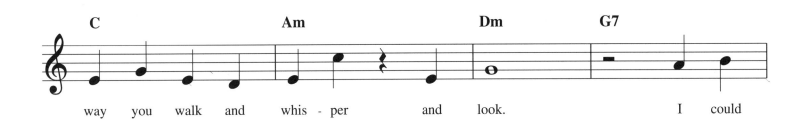

way you walk and whis - per and look. I could

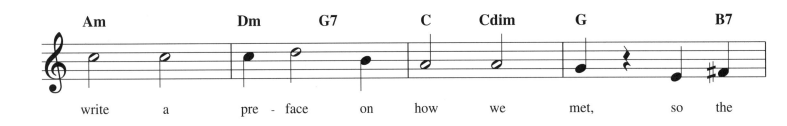

write a pre - face on how we met, so the

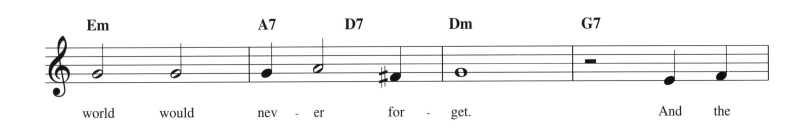

world would nev - er for - get. And the

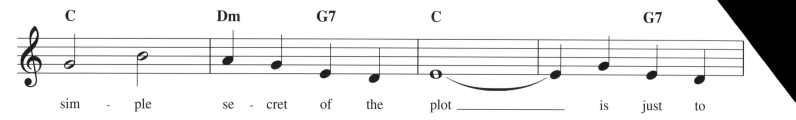

sim - ple   se - cret of the   plot _____ is   just   to

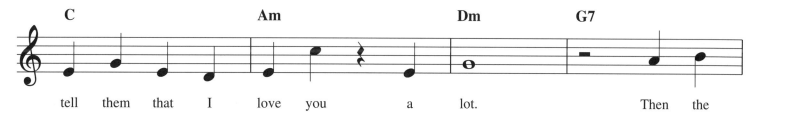

tell them that I   love you   a   lot.   Then the

world dis - cov - ers   as   my   book   ends,   how to

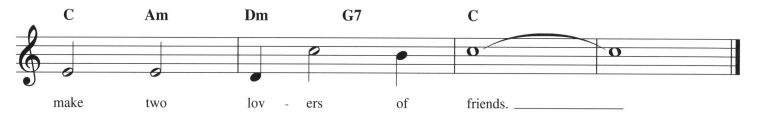

make   two   lov - ers   of   friends. _____

I'VE GOT YOU UNDER MY SKIN
from BORN TO DANCE

Words and Music by
COLE PORTER

IF EVER I WOULD LEAVE YOU
from CAMELOT

Words by ALAN JAY LERNER
Music by FREDERICK LOEWE

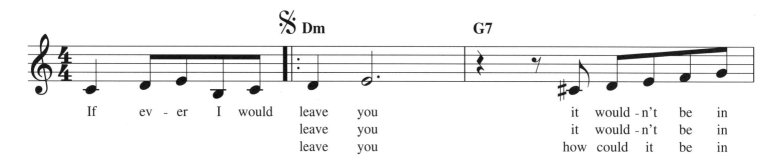

If ev - er I would leave you
it would -n't be in

leave you
it would -n't be in

leave you
how could it be in

sum - mer.
See - ing you in

au - tumn.
How I'd leave in

spring - time,
know - ing how in

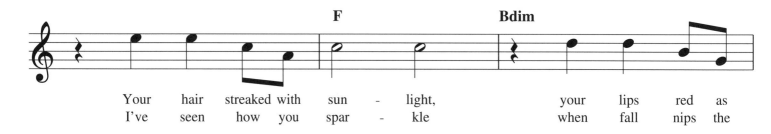

sum - mer I nev - er would go.

au - tumn I nev - er will know.

spring I'm be - witched by you so?

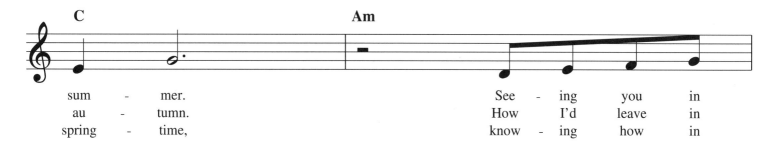

Your hair streaked with sun - light,
your lips red as

I've seen how you spar - kle
when fall nips the

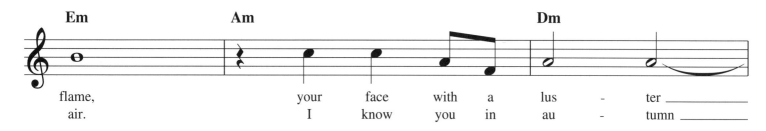

flame,
your face with a lus - ter ____

air.
I know you in au - tumn ____

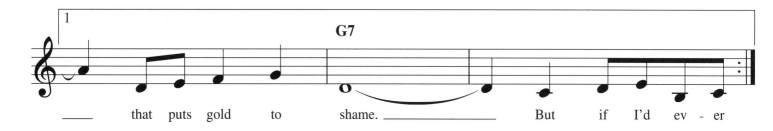

____ that puts gold to shame. ____ But if I'd ev - er

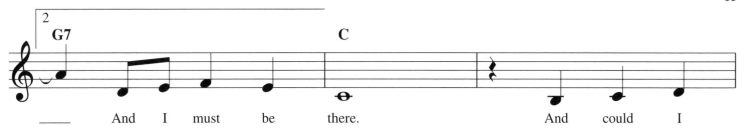

G7　　　　　　　　　　　　　　　　　　**C**

_____ And I must be there.　　　And could I

E　　　　　**C♯m**　　　　　**F♯m**　　　　　**B7**

leave you run - ning mer - ri - ly through the

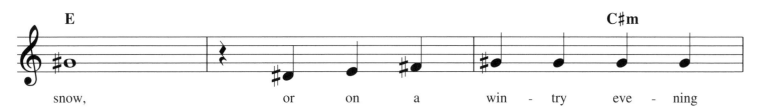

E　　　　　　　　　　　　　　　　　　**C♯m**

snow,　　　or on a win - try eve - ning

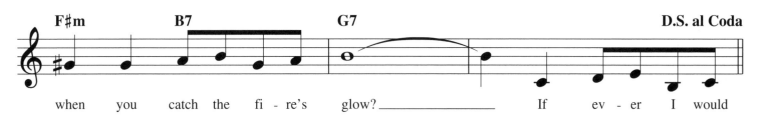

F♯m　　　**B7**　　　　**G7**　　　　　　　**D.S. al Coda**

when you catch the fi - re's glow? _____ If ev - er I would

CODA

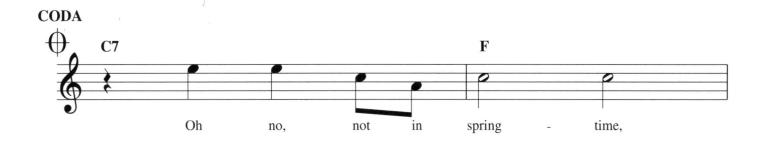

C7　　　　　　　　　　　　　　　　**F**

Oh no, not in spring - time,

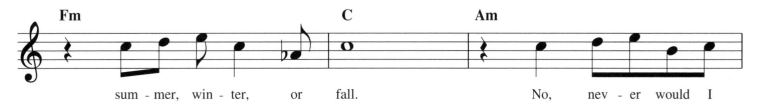

Fm　　　　　　　　　　**C**　　　**Am**

sum - mer, win - ter, or fall.　　No, nev - er would I

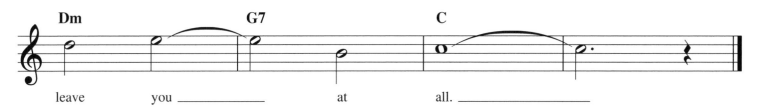

Dm　　　　　　　**G7**　　　　　　**C**

leave you _____ at all. _____

IF I HAD A HAMMER
(The Hammer Song)

Words and Music by LEE HAYS
and PETE SEEGER

Additional Lyrics

3. If I had a song,
   I'd sing it in the morning;
   I'd sing it in the evening
      all over this land;
   I'd sing out danger,
   I'd sing out a warning,
   I'd sing out love between my
      brothers and my sisters,
   All over this land.

4. Well, I got a hammer,
   And I've got a bell
   And I've got a song
      all over this land;
   It's the hammer of justice,
   It's the bell of freedom,
   It's the song about love
      between my brothers and my sisters,
   All over this land.

LET IT BE

Words and Music by JOHN LENNON
and PAUL McCARTNEY

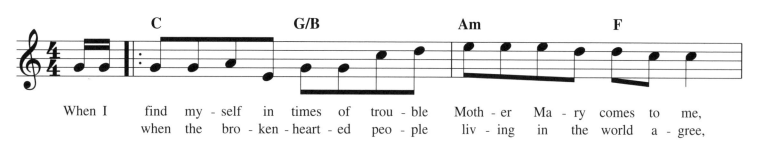

When I find my - self in times of trou - ble Moth - er Ma - ry comes to me,
when the bro - ken - heart - ed peo - ple liv - ing in the world a - gree,

speak - ing words of wis - dom, let it be. _____ And
there will be an an - swer, let it be. _____ For

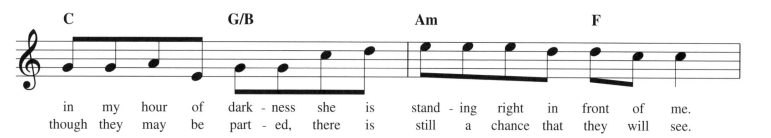

in my hour of dark - ness she is stand - ing right in front of me.
though they may be part - ed, there is still a chance that they will see.

Speak - ing words of wis - dom, let it be. _____ }
There will be an an - swer, let it be. _____ }   Let it

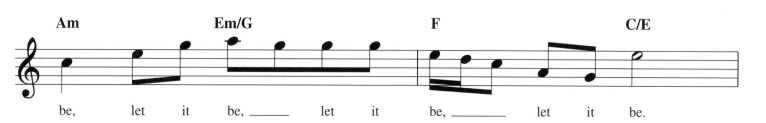

be, let it be, _____ let it be, _____ let it be.

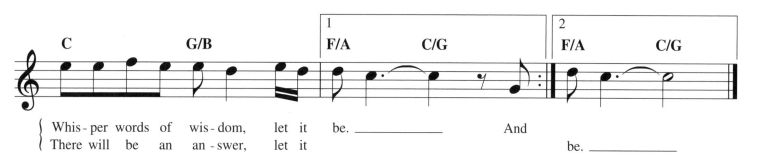

1.
F/A   C/G

2.
F/A   C/G

Whis - per words of wis - dom, let it be. _____ And
There will be an an - swer, let it

be. _____

IN THE STILL OF THE NIGHT
from ROSALIE

Words and Music by
COLE PORTER

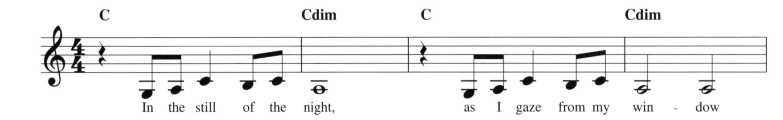

In the still of the night, as I gaze from my win - dow

at the moon in its flight my thoughts all stray to you. ___

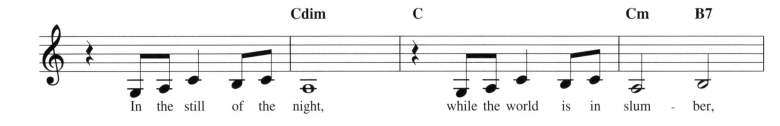

In the still of the night, while the world is in slum - ber,

oh, the times with - out num - ber, dar - ling, when I say to you: ___

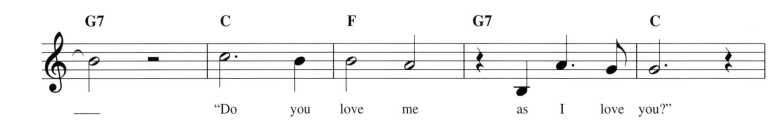

___ "Do you love me as I love you?"

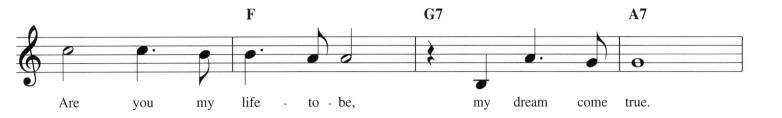

Are you my life - to - be, my dream come true.

Or will this dream of mine fade out of sight like the

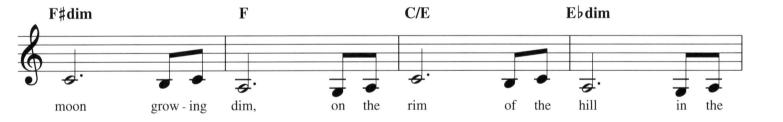

moon grow - ing dim, on the rim of the hill in the

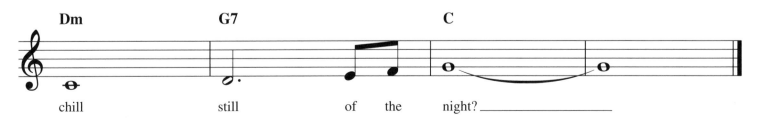

chill still of the night?

ISN'T IT ROMANTIC?
from the Paramount Picture LOVE ME TONIGHT

Words by LORENZ HART
Music by RICHARD RODGERS

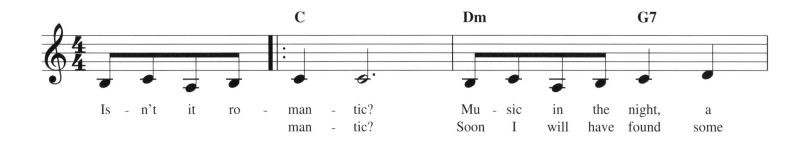

Is - n't it ro - man - tic? Mu - sic in the night, a
man - tic? Soon I will have found some

dream that can be heard. Is - n't it ro - man - tic?
girl that I a - dore. Is - n't it ro - man - tic?

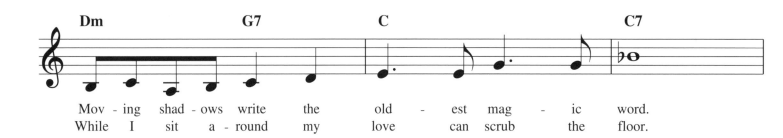

Mov - ing shad - ows write the old - est mag - ic word.
While I sit a - round my love can scrub the floor.

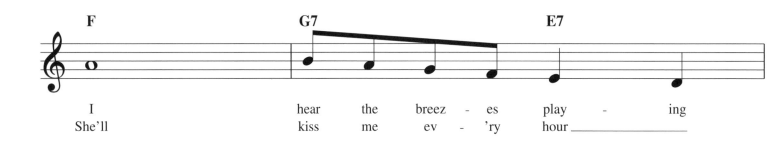

I hear the breez - es play - ing
She'll kiss me ev - 'ry hour

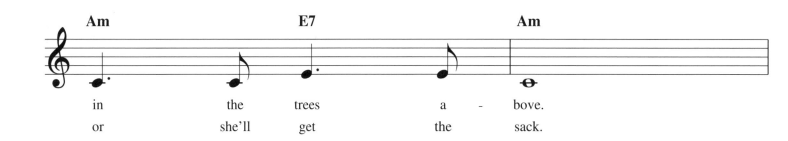

in the trees a - bove.
or she'll get the sack.

IT ONLY TAKES A MOMENT

from HELLO, DOLLY!

Music and Lyric by
JERRY HERMAN

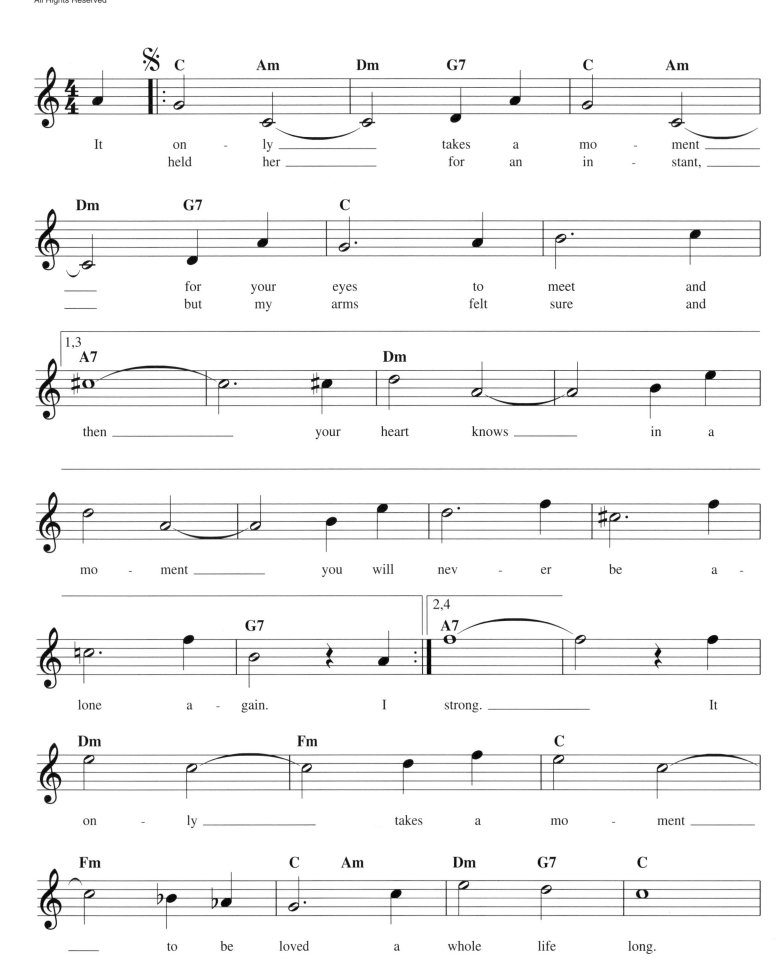

LEAVING ON A JET PLANE

Words and Music by
JOHN DENVER

tell me that ___ you'll wait for me, ___ hold me like ___ you'll

nev - er let me go. _____ 'Cause I'm leav - in'

on a jet ___ plane, don't know when I'll be back ___ a - gain, ___

1, 2

oh, babe, I hate to go. _____

3

2. There's so go. _____ I'm

3. _____

leav - in' on a jet ___ plane, don't know when I'll be back ___ a - gain, ___

oh, babe, _____ I hate to go. _____

_____ (Instrumental)

LOVE IS THE SWEETEST THING

Words and Music by
RAY NOBLE

LOVE ME TENDER

Words an

96

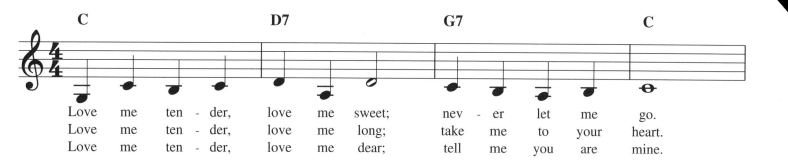

Love me ten - der, love me sweet; nev - er let me go.
Love me ten - der, love me long; take me to your heart.
Love me ten - der, love me dear; tell me you are mine.

You have made my life com - plete; and I love you so.
For it's there that I be - long, and we'll nev - er so part.
I'll be yours through all the year, 'til the end of time.

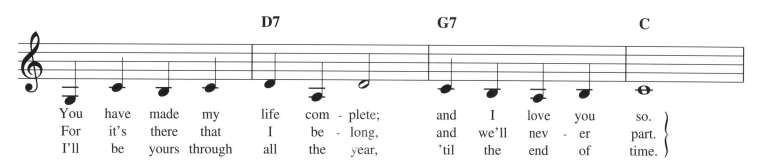

Love me ten - der, love me true; all my dreams ful -

fill. For, my dar - lin', I love you,

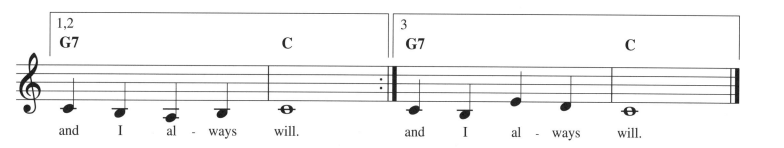

and I al - ways will. and I al - ways will.

LOVER MAN

(Oh, Where Can You Be?)

By JIMMY DAVIS,
ROGER "RAM" RAMIREZ and JIMMY SHERMAN

I don't know why, but I'm feel-ing so sad. ____
The night is cold, and I'm so all a - lone. ____
Some day we'll meet and you'll dry all my tears. ____

I long to try some - thing I've nev - er had. ____
I'd give my soul just to call you my own. ____
Then whis - per sweet lit - tle things in my ears. ____

Nev - er had no kiss - in', oh, what I've been miss - in'.
Got a moon a - bove me, but no one to love me.
Hug - gin' and a - kiss - in', oh, what I've been miss - in'.

Lov - er man, oh where can you be?

Fine

I've heard it said that the

thrill of ro - mance can be like a heav - en - ly dream.

D.C. al Fine

I go to bed with a pray'r that you'll make love to me, strange as it seems.

MANHATTAN
from the Broadway Musical THE GARRICK GAIETIES

Words by LORENZ HART
Music by RICHARD RODGERS

MARIA
from THE SOUND OF MUSIC

Lyrics by OSCAR HAMMERSTEIN II
Music by RICHARD RODGERS

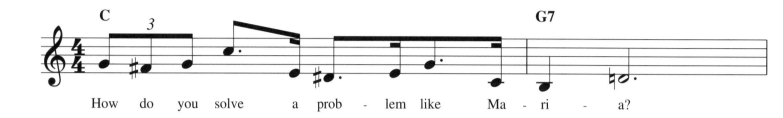

How do you solve a prob - lem like Ma - ri - a?

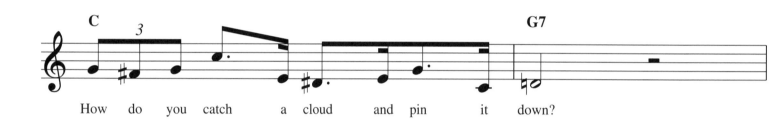

How do you catch a cloud and pin it down?

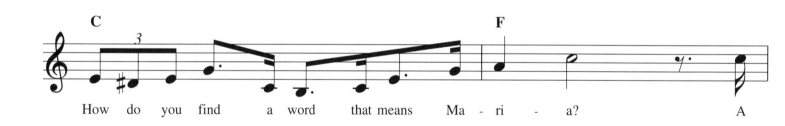

How do you find a word that means Ma - ri - a? A

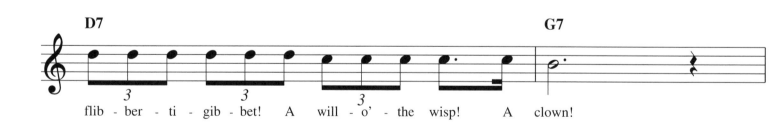

flib - ber - ti - gib - bet! A will - o' - the wisp! A clown!

Man - y a thing you know you'd like to tell her;

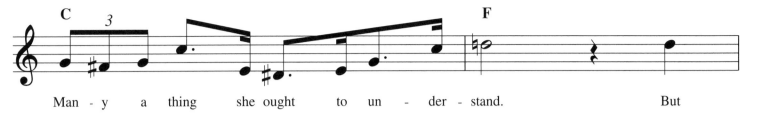

Man - y a thing she ought to un - der - stand. But

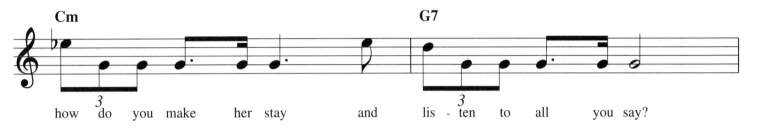

how do you make her stay and lis - ten to all you say?

How do you keep a wave up - on the sand? Oh,

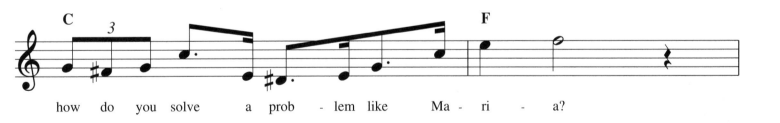

how do you solve a prob - lem like Ma - ri - a?

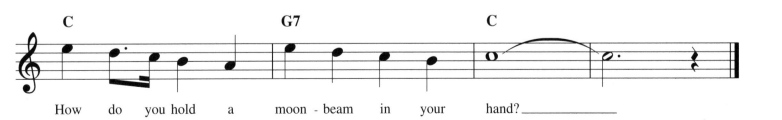

How do you hold a moon - beam in your hand?_____

MARIA ELENA

English Words by S.K. RUSSELL
Music and Spanish Words by LORENZO BARCELATA

MY HEART STOOD STILL
from A CONNECTICUT YANKEE

Words by LORENZ HART
Music by RICHARD RODGERS

MOOD INDIGO
from SOPHISTICATED LADIES

Words and Music by DUKE ELLINGTON,
IRVING MILLS and ALBANY BIGARD

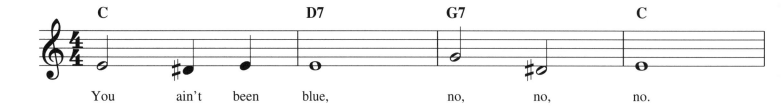

You ain't been blue, no, no, no.

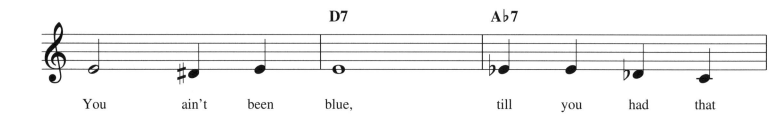

You ain't been blue, till you had that

mood in - di - go. That feel - in' goes steal - in'

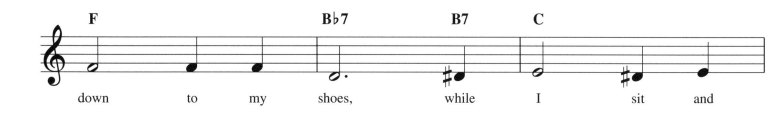

down to my shoes, while I sit and

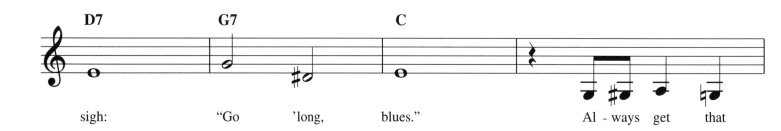

sigh: "Go 'long, blues." Al - ways get that

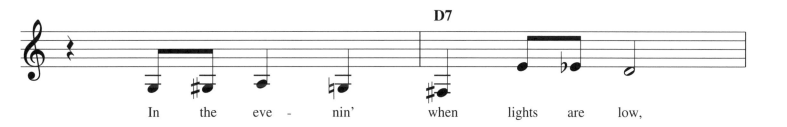

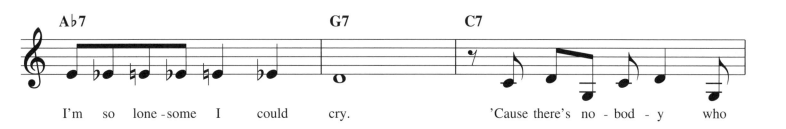

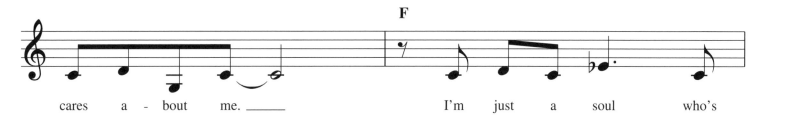

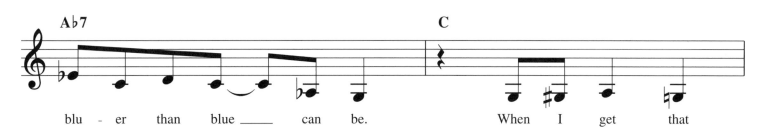

MY FAVORITE THINGS
from THE SOUND OF MUSIC

Lyrics by OSCAR HAMMERSTEIN II
Music by RICHARD RODGERS

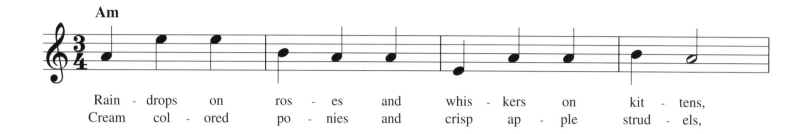

Rain - drops on ros - es and whis - kers on kit - tens,
Cream col - ored po - nies and crisp ap - ple strud - els,

bright cop - per ket - tles and warm wool - en mit - tens,
door - bells and sleigh - bells and schnitz - el with noo - dles,

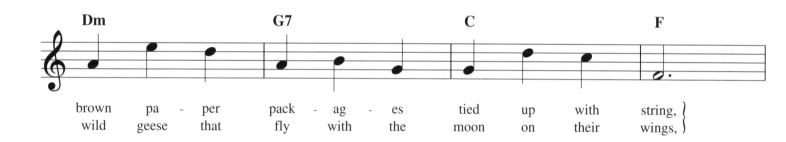

brown pa - per pack - ag - es tied up with string,
wild geese that fly with the moon on their wings,

these are a few of my fa - vor - ite things.

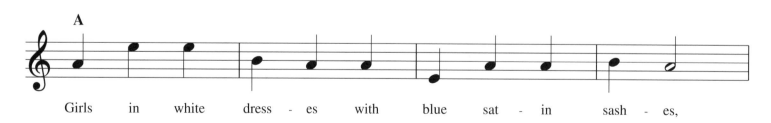

Girls in white dress - es with blue sat - in sash - es,

snow - flakes that stay on my nose and eye - lash - es,

MY FUNNY VALENTINE
from BABES IN ARMS

Words by LORENZ HART
Music by RICHARD RODGERS

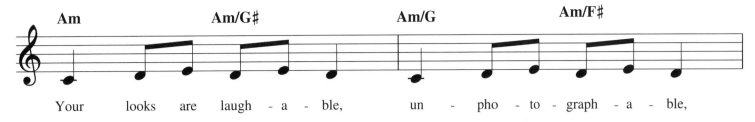

Your looks are laugh - a - ble, un - pho - to - graph - a - ble,

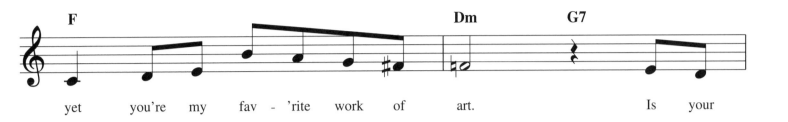

yet you're my fav - 'rite work of art. Is your

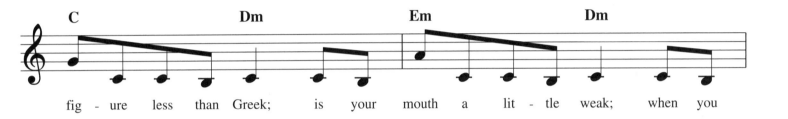

fig - ure less than Greek; is your mouth a lit - tle weak; when you

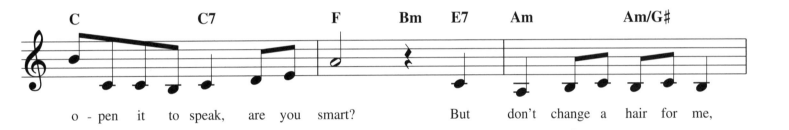

o - pen it to speak, are you smart? But don't change a hair for me,

not if you care for me. Stay, lit - tle Val - en - tine,

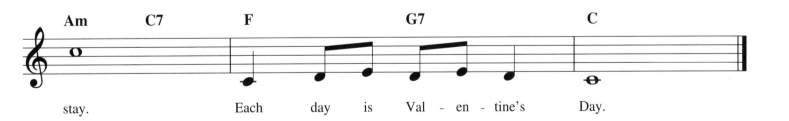

stay. Each day is Val - en - tine's Day.

MY MELANCHOLY BABY

Words by GEORGE NORTON
Music by ERNIE BURNETT

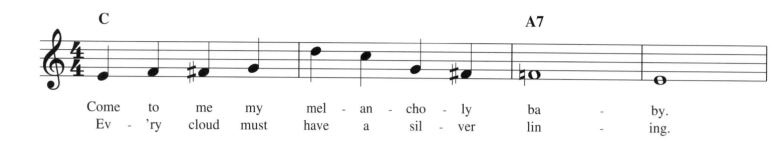

Come to me my mel - an - cho - ly ba - - by.
Ev - 'ry cloud must have a sil - ver lin - - ing.

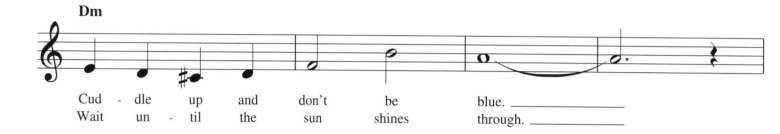

Cud - dle up and don't be blue. _____
Wait un - til the sun be shines through. _____

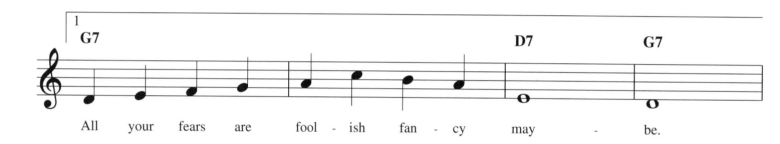

All your fears are fool - ish fan - cy may - be.

You know, dear, that I'm in love with you. _____

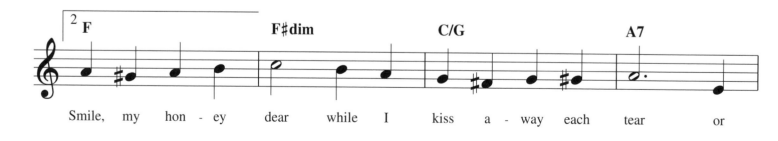

Smile, my hon - ey dear while I kiss a - way each tear or

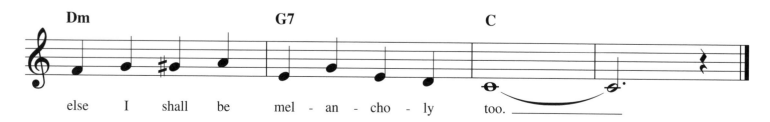

else I shall be mel - an - cho - ly too. _____

NO OTHER LOVE

from ME AND JULIET

Lyrics by OSCAR HAMMERSTEIN II
Music by RICHARD RODGERS

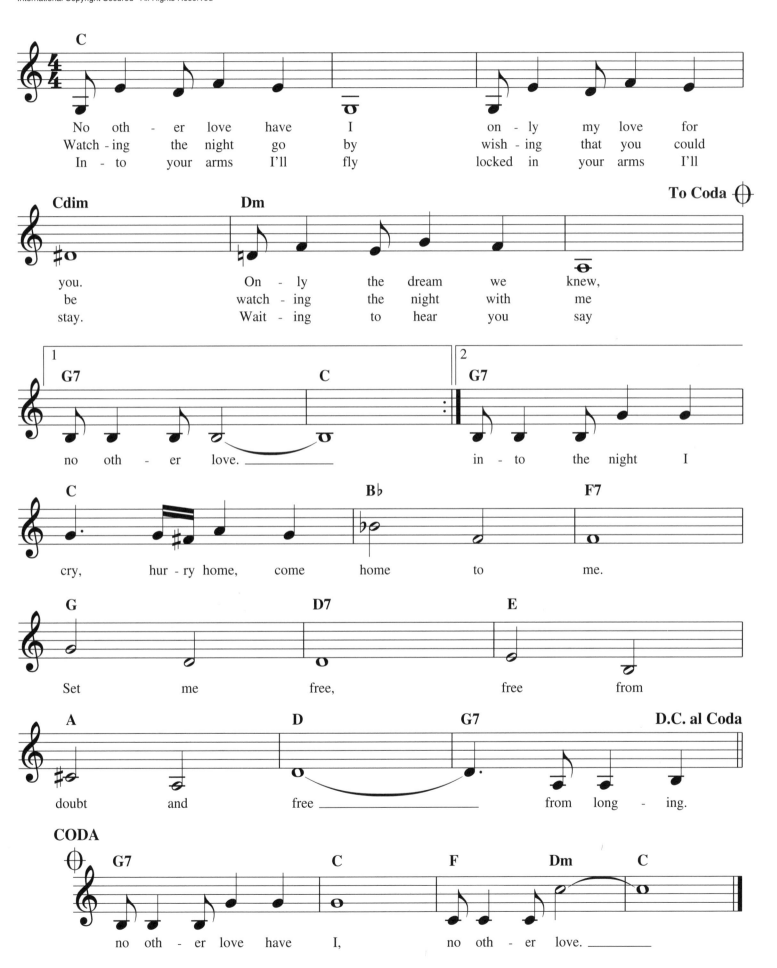

MY ROMANCE
from JUMBO

Words by LORENZ HART
Music by RICHARD RODGERS

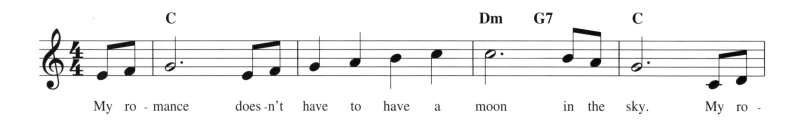

My ro - mance does -n't have to have a moon in the sky. My ro -

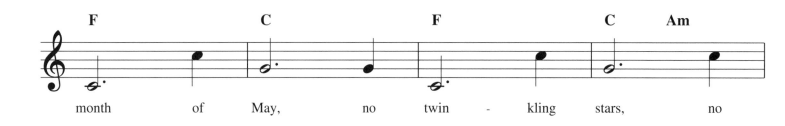

mance does -n't need a blue la - goon stand -ing by; no

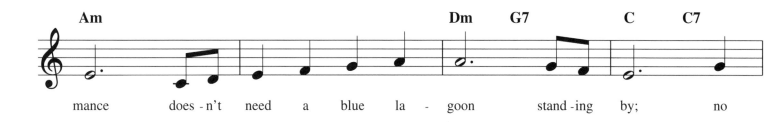

month of May, no twin - kling stars, no

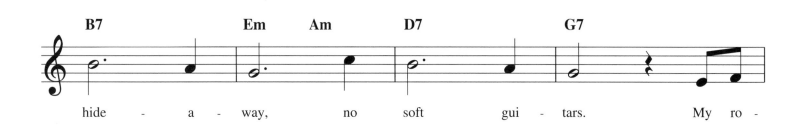

hide - a - way, no soft gui - tars. My ro -

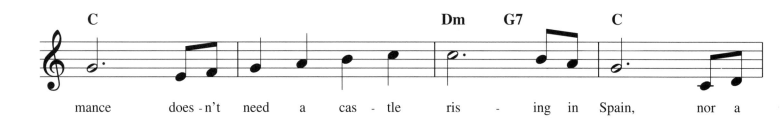

mance does -n't need a cas - tle ris - ing in Spain, nor a

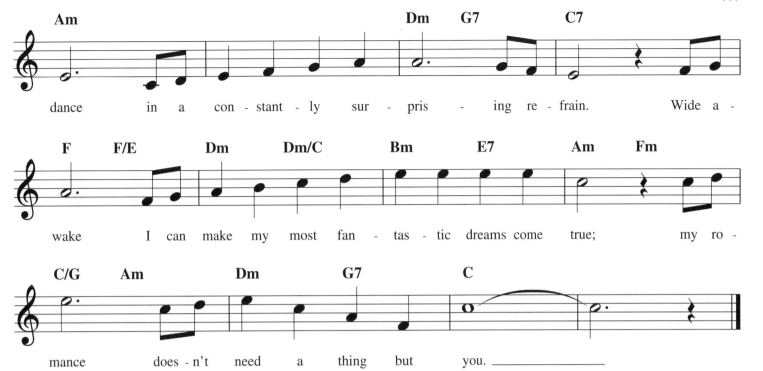

dance in a con-stant-ly sur-pris-ing re-frain. Wide a-wake I can make my most fan-tas-tic dreams come true; my ro-mance does-n't need a thing but you._____

PREPARE YE
(The Way of the Lord)
from the Musical GODSPELL

Words and Music by
STEPHEN SCHWARTZ

Pre - pare ye ___ the way of ___ the Lord.

Pre - pare ye ___ the way of ___ the Lord.

Pre - pare ye ___ the way of ___ the Lord.

Pre - pare ye ___ the way of ___ the Lord.

NEVER ON SUNDAY

Words by BILLY TOWNE
Music by MANOS HADJIDAKIS

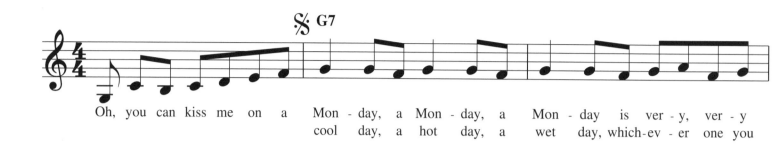

Oh, you can kiss me on a Mon - day, a Mon - day, a Mon - day is ver - y, ver - y
cool day, a hot day, a wet day, which-ev - er one you

good.
choose.
Or you can kiss me on a Tues - day, a Tues - day, a
Or try to kiss me on a gray day, a May day, a

Tues - day, in fact I wish you would.
pay day, and see if I re - fuse.
Or you can kiss me on a
And if you make it on a

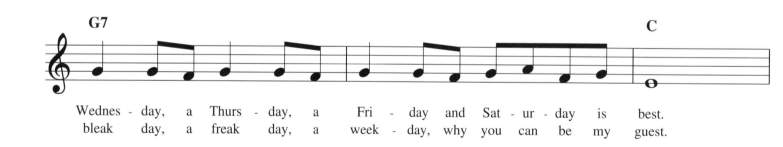

Wednes - day, a Thurs - day, a Fri - day and Sat - ur - day is best.
bleak day, a freak day, a week - day, why you can be my guest.

To Coda

But nev - er, nev - er on a Sun - day, a Sun - day, a Sun - day, 'cause that's my day to
But nev - er, nev - er on a Sun - day, a Sun - day, the one day I need a lit - tle

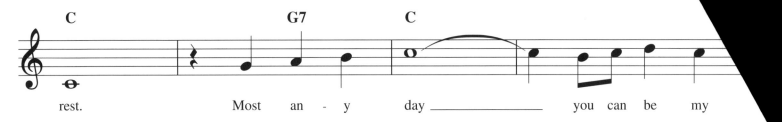

rest.   Most   an - y   day _____ you   can   be   my

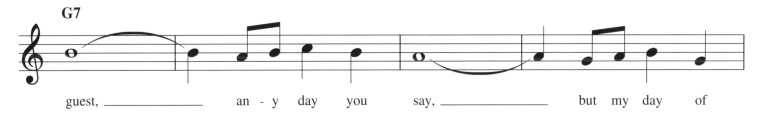

guest, _____ an - y   day   you   say, _____ but   my   day   of

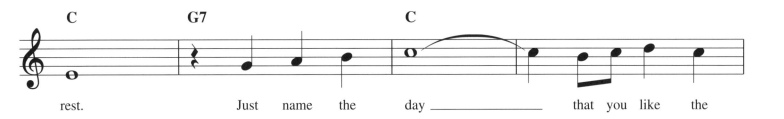

rest.   Just   name   the   day _____ that   you   like   the

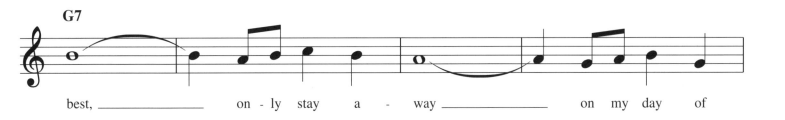

best, _____ on - ly   stay   a - way _____ on   my   day   of

CODA

rest.   Oh,   you   can   kiss   me   on   a

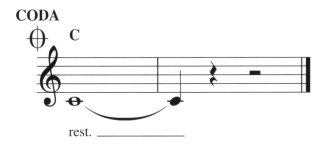

rest. _____

OH, WHAT A BEAUTIFUL MORNIN'
from OKLAHOMA!

Words by OSCAR HAMMERSTEIN II
Music by RICHARD RODGERS

113

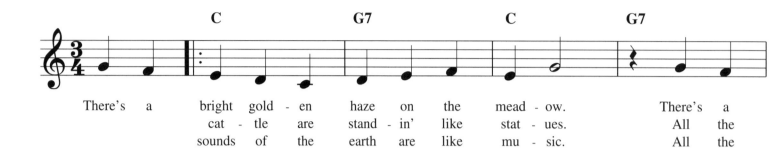

There's a bright gold - en haze on the mead - ow. There's a
cat - tle are stand - in' like stat - ues. All the
sounds of the earth are like mu - sic. All the

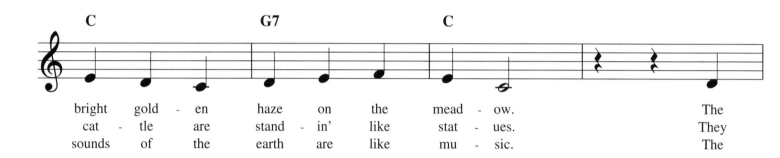

bright gold - en haze on the mead - ow. The
cat - tle are stand - in' like stat - ues. They
sounds of the earth are like mu - sic. The

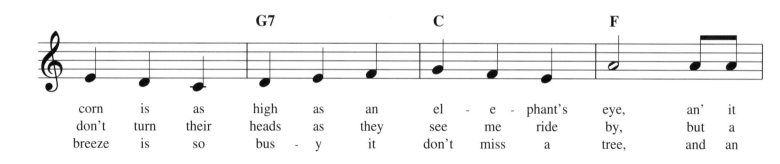

corn is as high as an el - e - phant's eye, an' it
don't turn their heads as they see me ride by, but a
breeze is so bus - y it don't miss a tree, and an

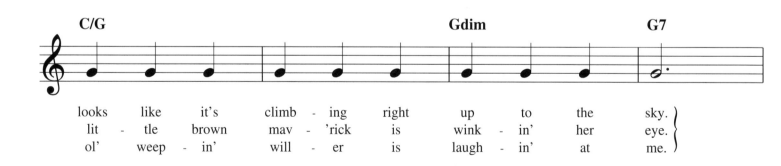

looks like it's climb - ing right up to the sky.
lit - tle brown mav - 'rick is wink - in' her eye.
ol' weep - in' will - er is laugh - in' at me.

Oh, what a beau - ti - ful morn - in',

oh, what a beau - ti - ful day. _____

I got a beau - ti - ful feel - in'

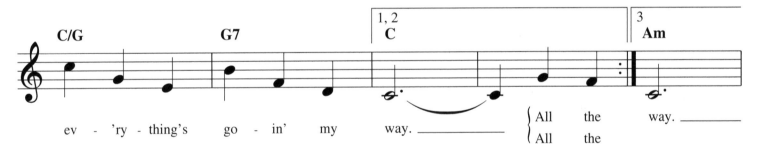

ev - 'ry - thing's go - in' my way. _____ { All the way. _____ { All the

____ Oh, what a beau - ti - ful day. _____

OKLAHOMA
from OKLAHOMA!

Lyrics by OSCAR HAMMERSTEIN II
Music by RICHARD RODGERS

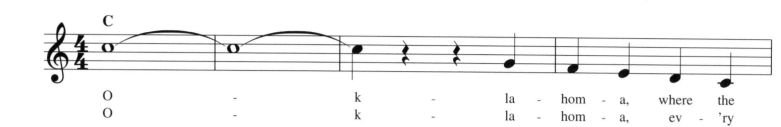

O - k - la - hom - a, where the
O - k - la - hom - a, ev - 'ry

wind comes sweep - in' down the plain _____ And the
night my hon - ey lamb and I _____ Sit a -

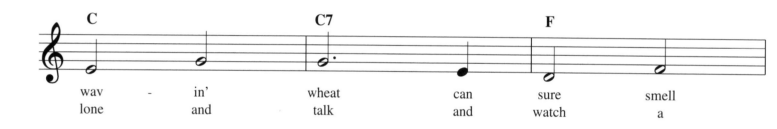

wav - in' wheat can sure smell
lone and talk and watch a

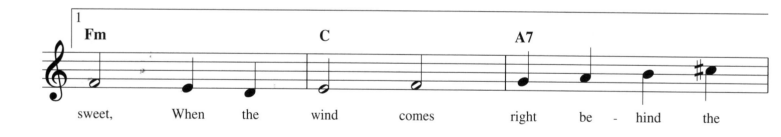

sweet, When the wind comes right be - hind the

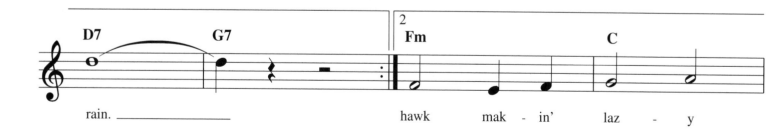

rain. _____ hawk mak - in' laz - y

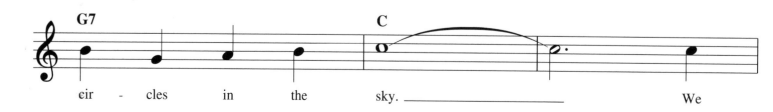

cir - cles in the sky. _____ We

OL' MAN RIVER
from SHOWBOAT

International Publishing, Inc.

Lyrics by OSCAR HAMMERSTEIN II
Music by JEROME KERN

Ol' Man Riv - er 'dat Ol' Man Riv - er, he must know sump - in' but

don't say noth - in'. He jus' keeps roll - in', he keeps on roll - in' a -

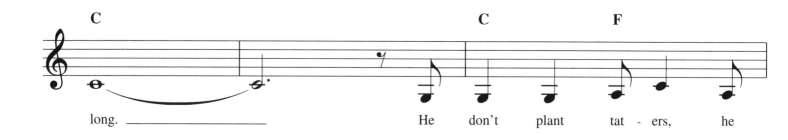

long. _____ He don't plant tat - ers, he

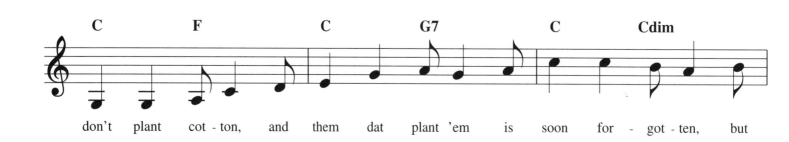

don't plant cot - ton, and them dat plant 'em is soon for - got - ten, but

Ol' Man Riv - er, he just keeps roll - in' a - long. _____

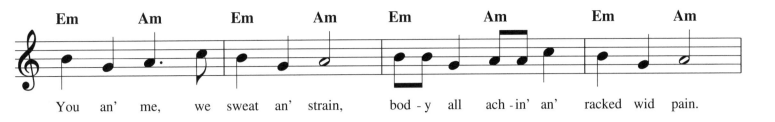

You an' me, we sweat an' strain, bod - y all ach - in' an' racked wid pain.

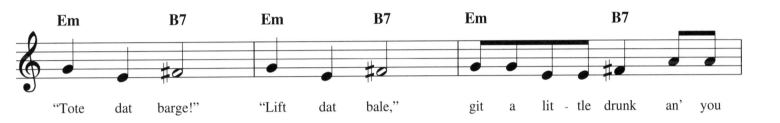

"Tote dat barge!" "Lift dat bale," git a lit - tle drunk an' you

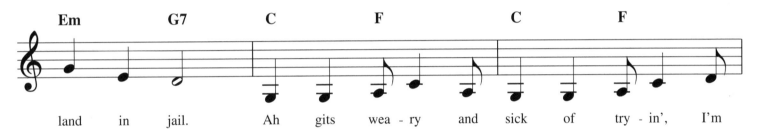

land in jail. Ah gits wea - ry and sick of try - in', I'm

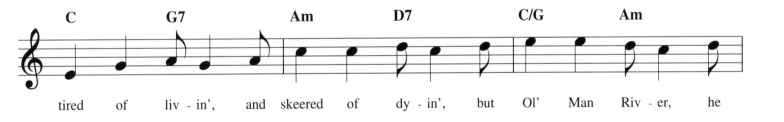

tired of liv - in', and skeered of dy - in', but Ol' Man Riv - er, he

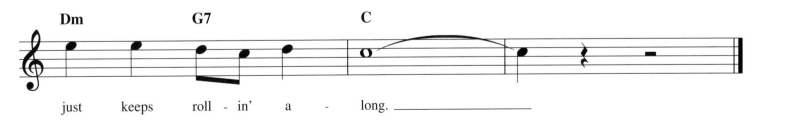

just keeps roll - in' a - long.

ON THE STREET WHERE YOU LIVE

from MY FAIR LADY

Words by ALAN JAY LERNER
Music by FREDERICK LOEWE

the tow - er - ing feel - ing, _____ just to

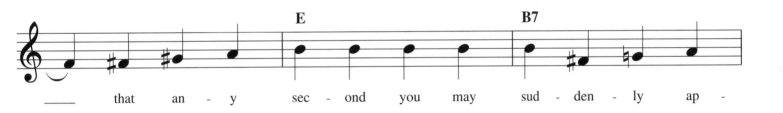

know _____ some - how you are near. _____ The

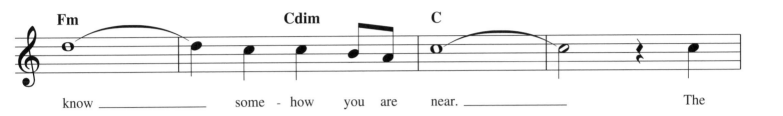

o - ver pow - er - ing feel - ing _____

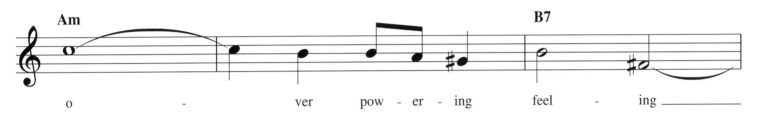

_____ that an - y sec - ond you may sud - den - ly ap -

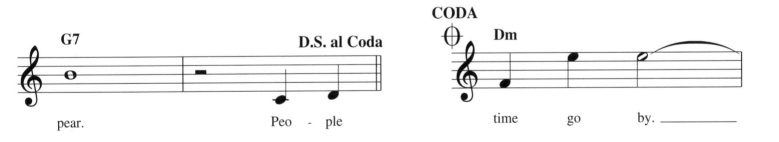

pear. Peo - ple time go by. _____

_____ I won't care if I _____ can be

here on the street where you live. _____

RAINDROPS KEEP FALLIN' ON MY HEAD
from BUTCH CASSIDY AND THE SUNDANCE KID

Lyric by HAL DAVID
Music by BURT BACHARACH

SATIN DOLL
from SOPHISTICATED LADIES

Words by JOHNNY MERCER and BILLY STRAYHORN
Music by DUKE ELLINGTON

SEVENTY SIX TROMBONES
from Meredith Willson's THE MUSIC MAN

By MEREDITH WILLSON

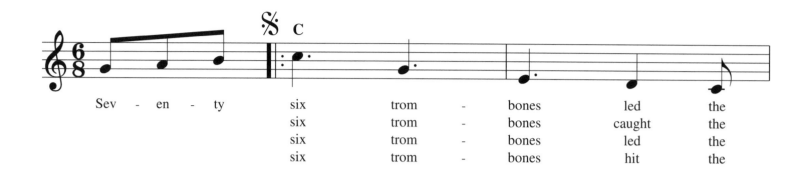

Sev - en - ty six trom - bones led the
six trom - bones caught the
six trom - bones led the
six trom - bones hit the

big pa - rade, _____ with a hun - dred and
morn - ing sun, _____ with a hun - dred and
big pa - rade, _____ when the or - der to
count - er - point, _____ while a hun - dred and

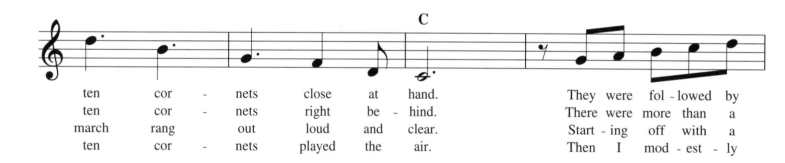

ten cor - nets close at hand. They were fol - lowed by
ten cor - nets right be - hind. There were more than a
march rang out loud and clear. Start - ing off with a
ten cor - nets played the air. Then I mod - est - ly

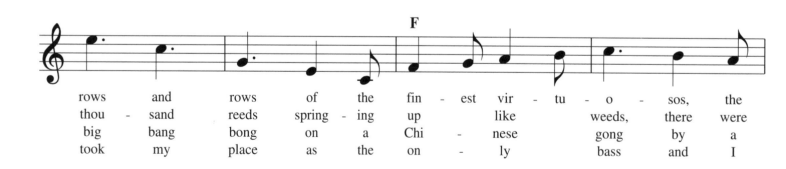

rows and rows of the fin - est vir - tu - o - sos, the
thou - sand reeds spring - ing up like weeds, there were
big bang bong on a Chi - nese gong by a
took my place as the on - ly bass and I

cream _____ of ev - 'ry fa - mous band. _____ Sev - en - ty
big _____ bang bong - er at the rear. _____ Sev - en - ty

SMOKE GETS IN YOUR EYES
from ROBERTA

Words by OTTO HARBACH
Music by JEROME KERN

STORMY WEATHER
(Keeps Rainin' All the Time)
from COTTON CLUB PARADE OF 1933

128

SOMEWHERE OUT THERE

from AN AMERICAN TAIL

Words and Music by JAMES HORNER,
BARRY MANN and CYNTHIA WEIL

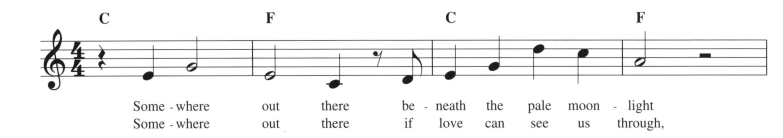

Some - where   out   there   be - neath   the   pale   moon - light
Some - where   out   there   if   love   can   see   us   through,

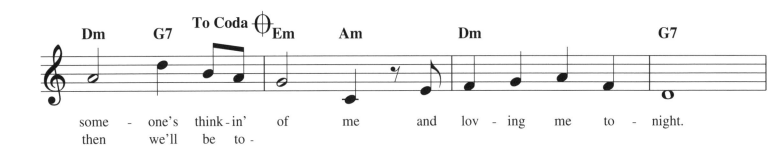

some - one's   think - in'   of   me   and   lov - ing   me   to - night.
then   we'll   be   to -

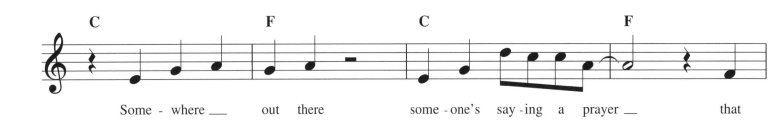

Some - where ___   out   there   some - one's   say - ing   a   prayer ___   that

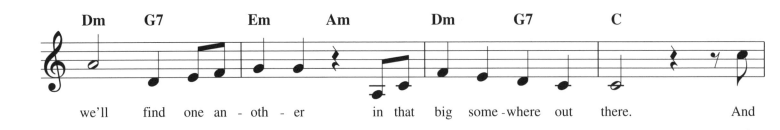

we'll   find   one   an - oth - er   in   that   big   some - where   out   there.   And

e - ven   though   I   know   how   ver - y   far   a - part   we   are,   it

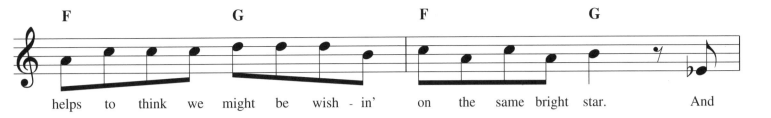

helps to think we might be wish - in' on the same bright star. And

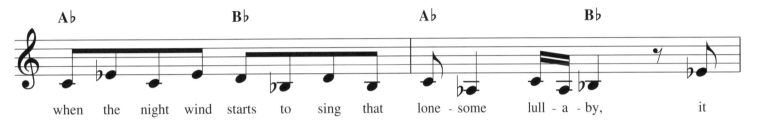

when the night wind starts to sing that lone - some lull - a - by, it

D.C. al Coda

helps to think we're sleep - ing un - der - neath the same big sky.

CODA

geth - er some - where out there, out where dreams come true.

SWANEE

Words by IRVING CAESAR
Music by GEORGE GERSHWIN

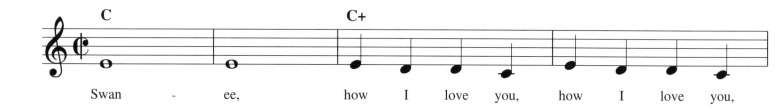

Swan - ee, how I love you, how I love you,

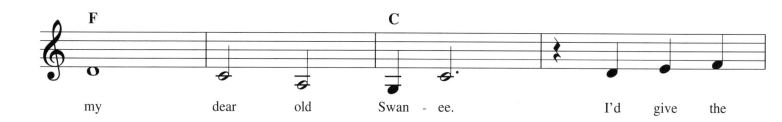

my dear old Swan - ee. I'd give the

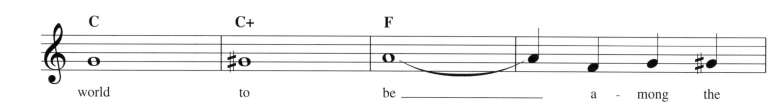

world to be _____ a - mong the

folks in D - I - X - I - E - ven know my

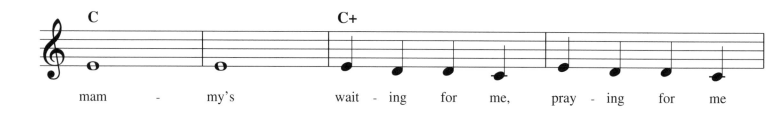

mam - my's wait - ing for me, pray - ing for me

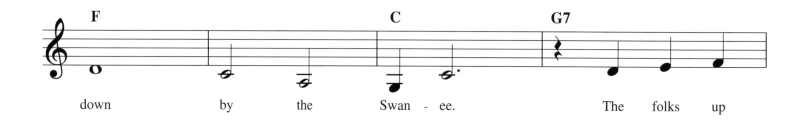

down by the Swan - ee. The folks up

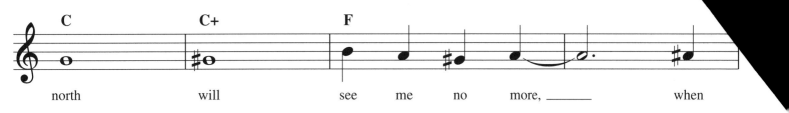

north   will   see   me   no   more, _____   when

Fine

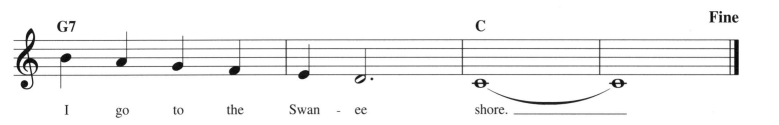

I   go   to   the   Swan - ee   shore. _____

Swan - ee, _____   Swan - ee, _____

____   I   am   com - ing   back   to

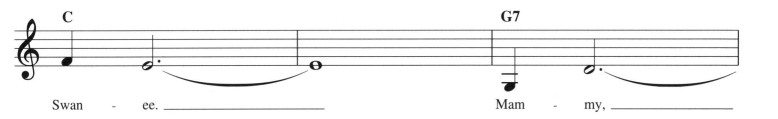

Swan - ee. _____   Mam - my, _____

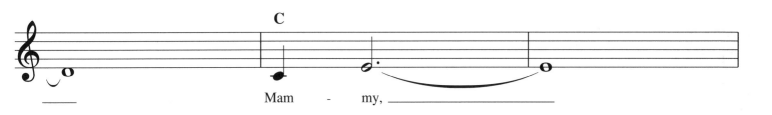

____   Mam - my, _____

D.C. al Fine

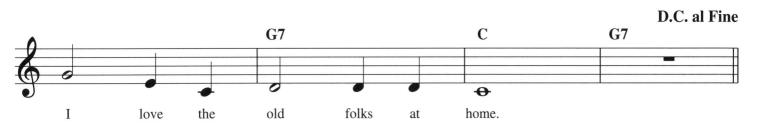

I   love   the   old   folks   at   home.

THAT OLD BLACK MAGIC
from the Paramount Picture STAR SPANGLED RHYTHM

Words by JOHNNY MERCER
Music by HAROLD ARLEN

THIS LAND IS YOUR LAND

Words and Music by
WOODY GUTHRIE

133

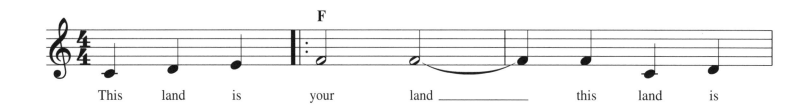

This land is your land _____ this land is

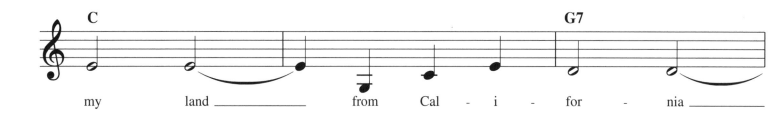

my land _____ from Cal - i - for - nia _____

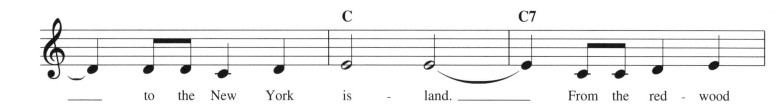

_____ to the New York is - land. _____ From the red - wood

for - est _____ to the Gulf Stream wa - ters; _____

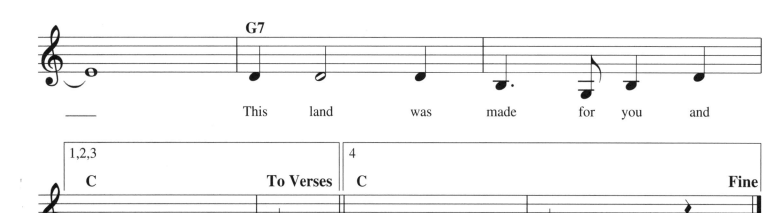

_____ This land was made for you and

me. | me. _____

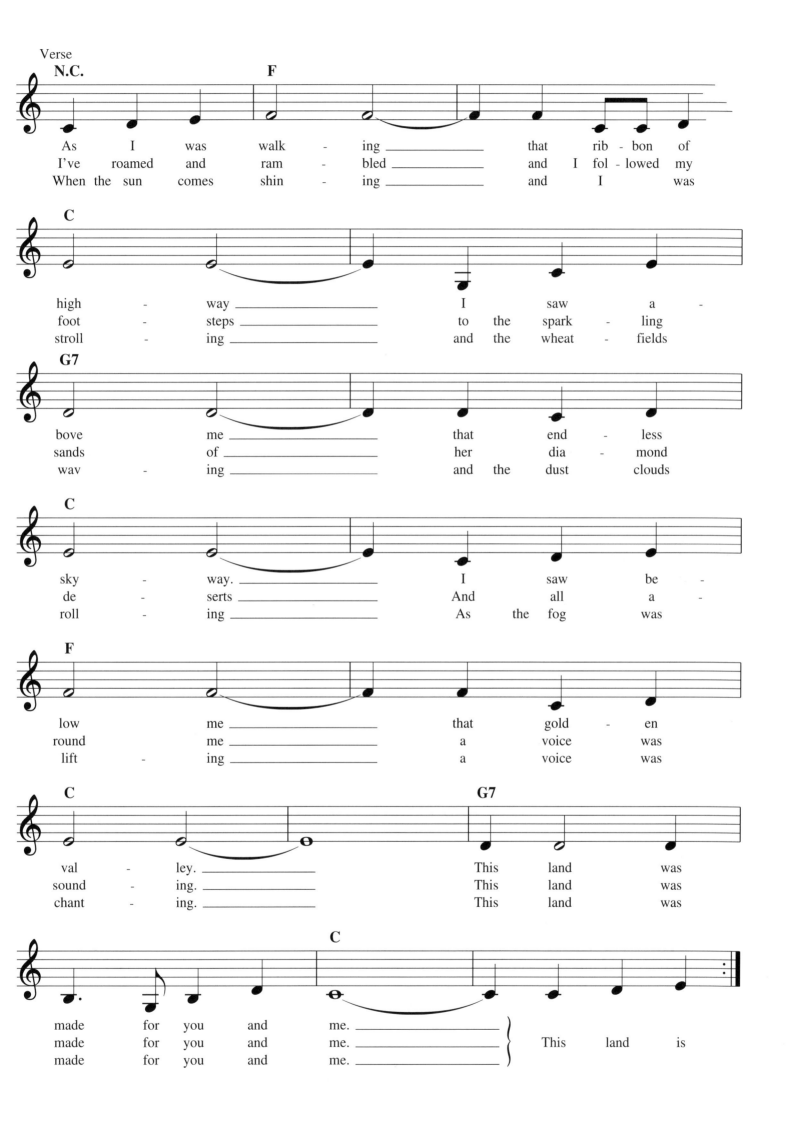

TILL THERE WAS YOU
from Meredith Willson's THE MUSIC MAN

By MEREDITH WILLSON

TOO LATE NOW

TRY TO REMEMBER
from THE FANTASTICKS

Words by TOM JONES
Music by HARVEY SCHMIDT

WALTZ FOR DEBBY

Lyric by GENE LEES
Music by BILL EVANS

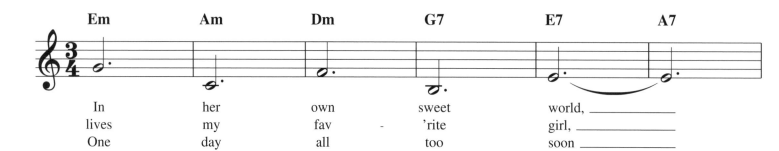

In her own sweet world, _____
lives my own fav - 'rite girl, _____
One day all too soon _____

pop - u - lat - ed by dolls and clowns and a
un - a - ware of the wor - ried frowns that we
she'll grow up and she'll leave her dolls and her

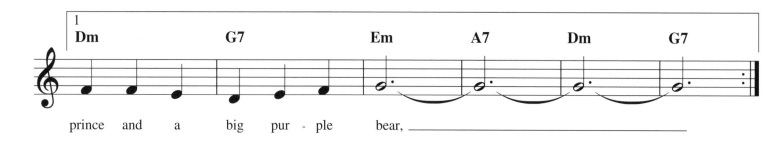

prince and a big pur - ple bear, _____

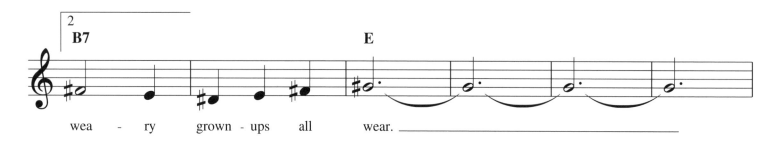

wea - ry grown - ups all wear. _____

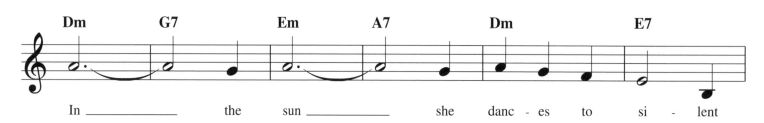

In _____ the sun _____ she danc - es to si - lent

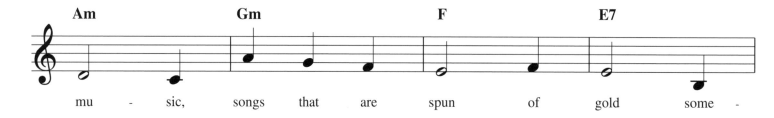

mu - sic, songs that are spun of gold some -

THE WAY YOU LOOK TONIGHT
from SWING TIME

Words by DOROTHY FIELDS
Music by JEROME KERN

Some - day when I'm aw - f'ly low,
love - ly, with your smile so warm
Love - ly, nev - er, nev - er change,

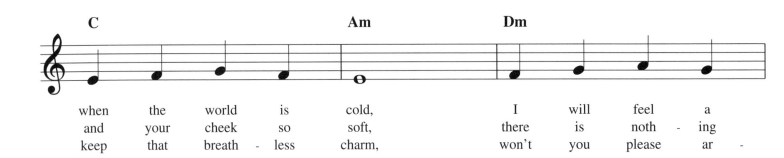

when the world is cold, I will feel a
and your cheek so soft, there is noth - ing
keep that breath - less charm, won't you please ar -

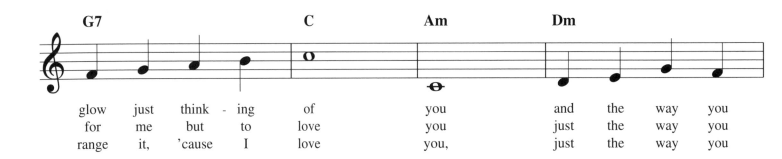

glow just think - ing of you and the way you
for me but to love you just the way you
range it, 'cause I love you, just the way you

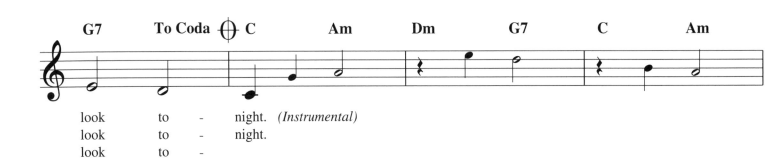

look to - night. (Instrumental)
look to - night.
look to -

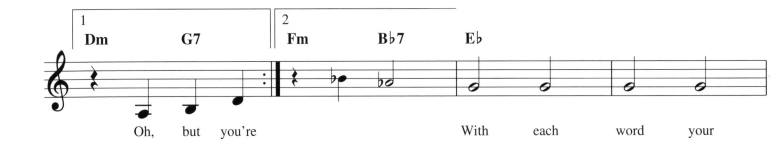

Oh, but you're   With each word your

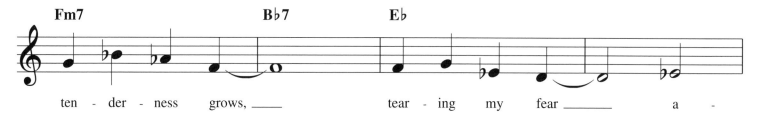

ten - der - ness grows, _____ tear - ing my fear _____ a -

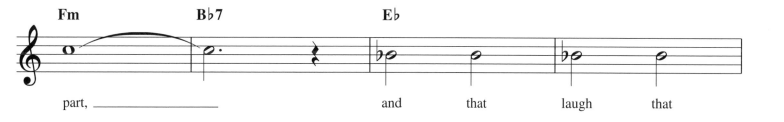

part, _____ and that laugh that

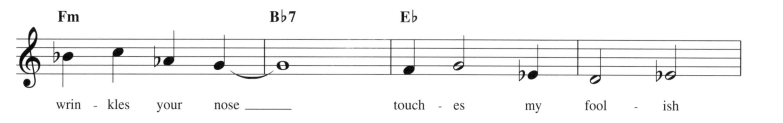

wrin - kles your nose _____ touch - es my fool - ish

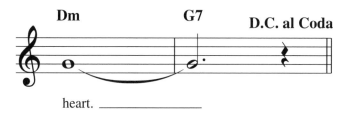

heart. _____

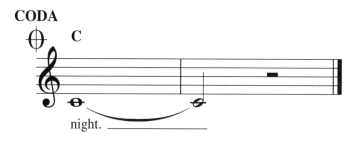

CODA

night. _____

WHAT KIND OF FOOL AM I?
from the Musical Production STOP THE WORLD - I WANT TO GET OFF

Words and Music by LESLIE BRICUSSE
and ANTHONY NEWLEY

WHEN THE SAINTS GO MARCHING IN

Words by KATHERINE E. PURVIS
Music by JAMES M. BLACK

WHEN I FALL IN LOVE
featured in the TriStar Motion Picture SLEEPLESS IN SEATTLE

Words by EDWARD HEYMAN
Music by VICTOR YOUNG

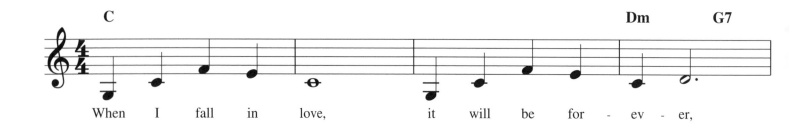

When I fall in love, it will be for - ev - er,

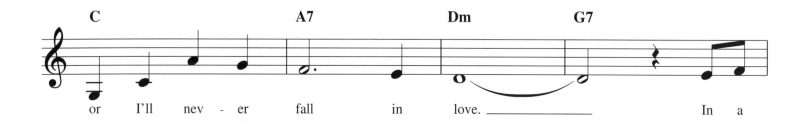

or I'll nev - er fall in love. _____ In a

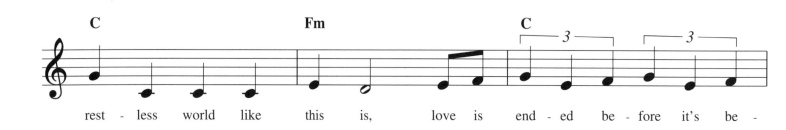

rest - less world like this is, love is end - ed be - fore it's be -

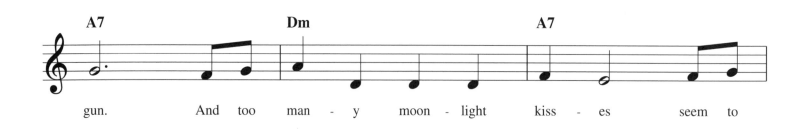

gun. And too man - y moon - light kiss - es seem to

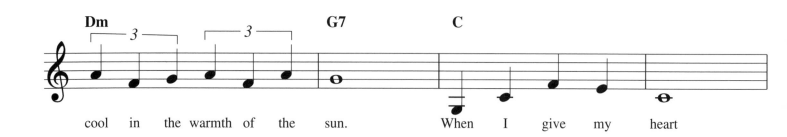

cool in the warmth of the sun. When I give my heart

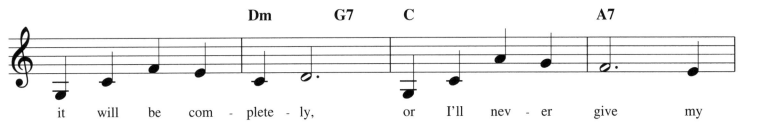

it will be com - plete - ly, or I'll nev - er give my

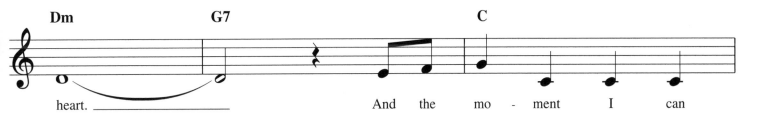

heart. _____ And the mo - ment I can

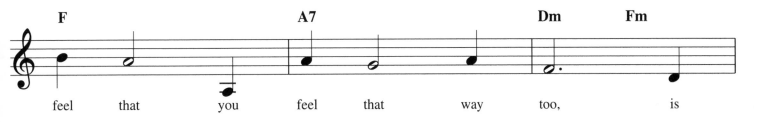

feel that you feel that way too, is

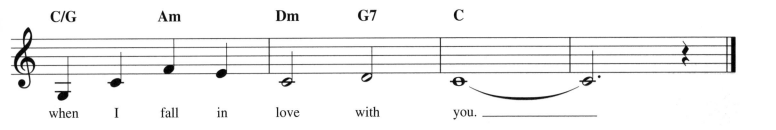

when I fall in love with you. _____

WHEN I'M SIXTY-FOUR
from YELLOW SUBMARINE

Words and Music by JOHN LENNON
and PAUL McCARTNEY

When I get old - er, los-ing my hair _ man - y years from now. _

Will you still be send-ing me a val - en - tine, _ birth - day greet - ings

bot - tle of wine? _ If I'd been out _ till quar - ter to three _

would you lock the door? _ Will you still need _ me,

will you still feed _ me when I'm six - ty - four?

Oo. _ You'll be

old - er, too. _ Ah, _

and if you say the word _ I could

stay with you. *(Instrumental)*

WHERE OR WHEN
from BABES IN ARMS

Words by LORENZ HART
Music by RICHARD RODGERS

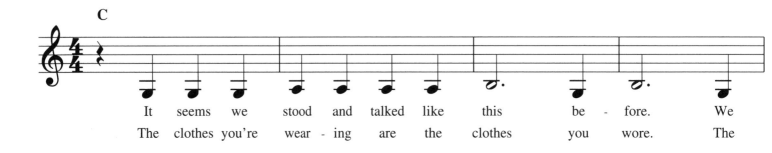

It seems we stood and talked like this be - fore. We
The clothes you're wear - ing are the clothes you wore. The

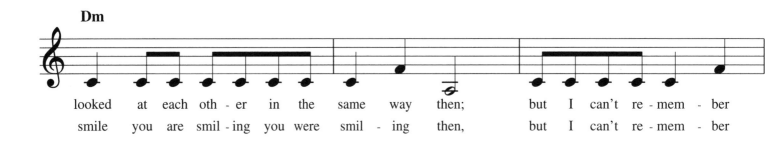

looked at each oth - er in the same way then; but I can't re - mem - ber
smile you are smil - ing you were smil - ing then, but I can't re - mem - ber

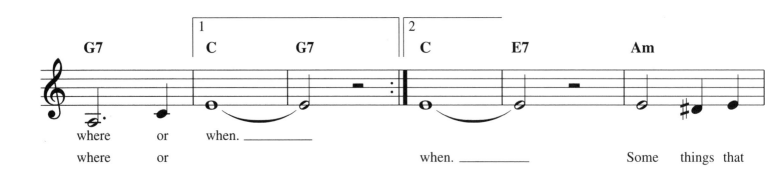

where or when. _____
where or   when. _____   Some things that

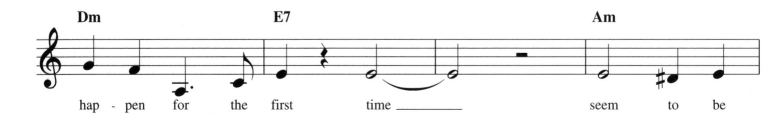

hap - pen for the first time _____   seem to be

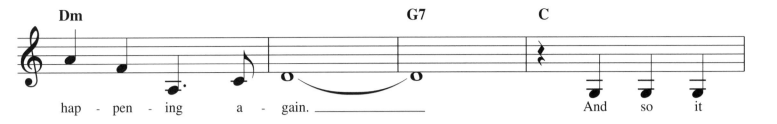

hap - pen - ing a - gain. _____ And so it

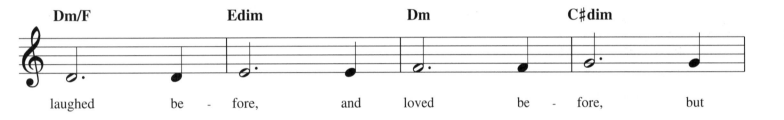

seems that we have met be - fore, and

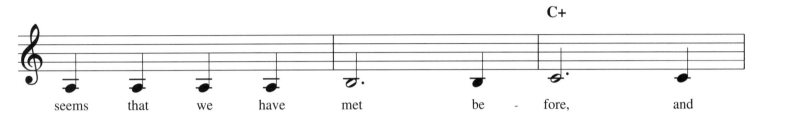

laughed be - fore, and loved be - fore, but

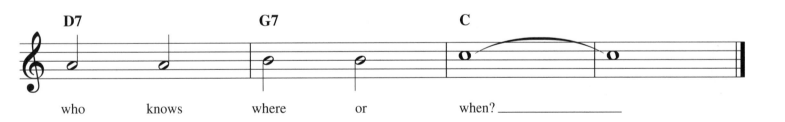

who knows where or when? _____

A WHOLE NEW WORLD
from Walt Disney's ALADDIN

Music by ALAN MENKEN
Lyrics by TIM RICE

YESTERDAY

Words and Music by JOHN LENNON
and PAUL McCARTNEY

YOU CAN DEPEND ON ME

Words and Music by CHARLES CARPENTER,
LOUIS DUNLAP and EARL HINES

YOU MADE ME LOVE YOU
(I Didn't Want to Do It)
from BROADWAY MELODY OF 1938

Words by JOE McCARTHY
Music by JAMES V. MONACO

YOUNG AT HEART

Words by CAROLYN LEIGH
Music by JOHNNY RICHARDS

Fair - y tales _____ can come true, _____ it can hap -pen to you if you're
know _____ that it's worth _____ ev - 'ry treas -ure on earth to be

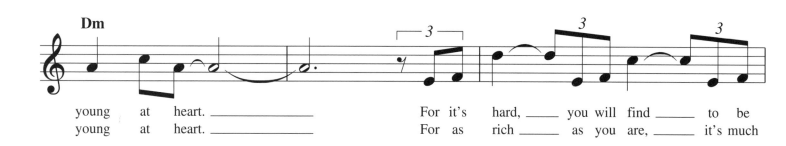

young at heart. _____ For it's hard, _____ you will find _____ to be
young at heart. _____ For as rich _____ as you are, _____ it's much

nar -row of mind if you're young at heart. _____ You can
bet -ter by far if you're young at heart. _____ And if

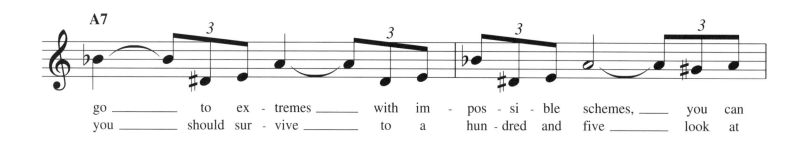

go _____ to ex - tremes _____ with im - pos -si -ble schemes, _____ you can
you _____ should sur - vive _____ to a hun -dred and five _____ look at

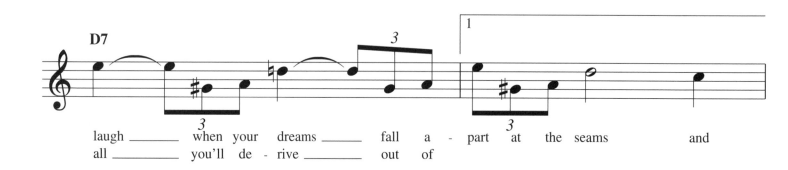

laugh _____ when your dreams _____ fall a -part at the seams and
all _____ you'll de -rive _____ out of

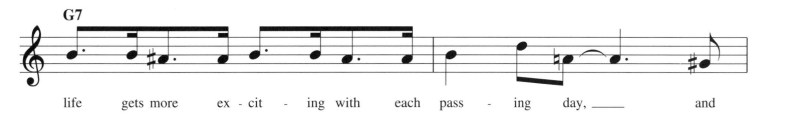

life gets more ex - cit - ing with each pass - ing day, _____ and

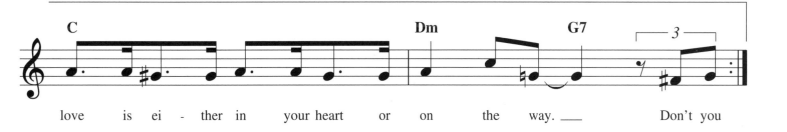

love is ei - ther in your heart or on the way. ___ Don't you

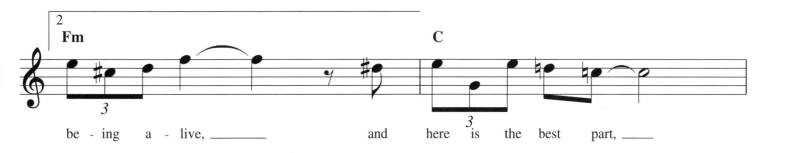

be - ing a - live, _____ and here is the best part, _____

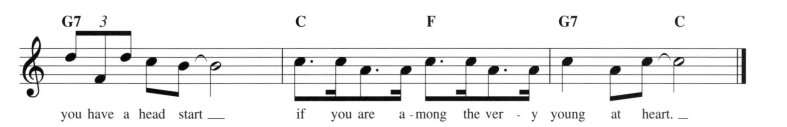

you have a head start ___ if you are a - mong the ver - y young at heart. _

YOU'RE NOBODY 'TIL SOMEBODY LOVES YOU

Words and Music by RUSS MORGAN,
LARRY STOCK and JAMES CAVANAUGH

THE ULTIMATE COLLECTION OF
FAKE BOOKS

The Ultimate Fake Book – 3rd Edition
Includes over 1,200 hits: Blue Skies • Body and Soul • Theme from Cheers • Endless Love • A Foggy Day • Isn't It Romantic? • Memory • Mona Lisa • Moon River • Operator • Piano Man • Roxanne • Satin Doll • Shout • Small World • Speak Softly, Love • Strawberry Fields Forever • Tears in Heaven • Unforgettable • hundreds more!

00240024 C Edition $45.00
00240026 B♭ Edition $45.00
00240025 E♭ Edition $45.00

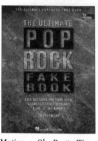

Best Fake Book Ever – 2nd Edition
More than 1000 songs from all styles of music, including: All My Loving • American Pie • At the Hop • Cabaret • Dust in the Wind • Fever • Free Bird • From a Distance • Hello, Dolly! • Hey Jude • King of the Road • Longer • Misty • Route 66 • Sentimental Journey • Somebody • Song Sung Blue • Spinning Wheel • Unchained Melody • We Will Rock You • What a Wonderful World • Wooly Bully • Y.M.C.A. • You're So Vain • and hundreds more.

00290239 C Edition $45.00
00240083 B♭ Edition $45.00
00240084 E♭ Edition $45.00

The Ultimate Pop/Rock Fake Book – 3rd Edition
Over 500 pop standards and contemporary hits, including: Addicted to Love • All Shook Up • Another One Bites the Dust • Crocodile Rock • Crying • Don't Know Much • Dust in the Wind • Earth Angel • Every Breath You Take • Hero • Hey Jude • Hold My Hand • Imagine • Layla • The Loco-Motion • Oh, Pretty Woman • On Broadway • Spinning Wheel • Stand by Me • Stayin' Alive • Tears in Heaven • True Colors • The Twist • Vision of Love • A Whole New World • Wild Thing • Wooly Bully • Yesterday • and many more!

00240099 $39.95

Latin Fake Book
Over 500 Latin songs in many styles, including mambos, sambas, cha cha chás, rhumbas, tangos, salsa, Latin pop and rock, and more. Songs include: Adiós • Água De Beber • Amapola • Antigua • Babalú • Bésame Mucho • Brazil • Cachita • Desafinado • Dindi • El Triste • Ella • Flamingo • Frenesí • The Girl from Ipanema • La Cucaracha • La Fiesta • Livin' La Vida Loca • Malagueña • Mambo No. 5 • Mambo No. 8 • Manteca • Maria Elena • One Note Samba • Poinciana • Similau • Spanish Eyes • Speak Low • St. Thomas • Tico Tico • Triste • Wave • more!

00240146 $35.00

The Ultimate Jazz Fake Book
Over 625 jazz classics spanning more than nine decades and representing all the styles of jazz. Includes: All of Me • All the Things You Are • Basin Street Blues • Birdland • Desafinado • A Foggy Day •I Concentrate on You • In the Mood • Take the "A" Train • Yardbird Suite • and many more!

00240079 C Edition $39.95
00240080 B♭ Edition $39.95
00240081 E♭ Edition $39.95

The Hal Leonard Real Jazz Book
A unique collection of jazz material in a wide variety of styles with no song duplication from *The Ultimate Jazz Fake Book!* Includes over 500 songs including a great deal of hard-to-find repertoire and a significant number of songs which have never before been printed.

00240097 C Edition $39.95
00240122 B♭ Edition $39.95
00240123 E♭ Edition $39.95

The Ultimate Broadway Fake Book – 4th Edition
More than 670 show-stoppers from over 200 shows! Includes: Ain't Misbehavin' • All I Ask of You • As If We Never Said Goodbye • Bewitched • Camelot • Memory • Don't Cry for Me Argentina • Edelweiss • I Dreamed a Dream • If I Were a Rich Man • Oklahoma • People • Seasons of Love • Send in the Clowns • Someone • What I Did for Love • and more.

00240046 $39.95

The Classical Fake Book
An unprecedented, amazingly comprehensive reference of over 650 classical themes and melodies for all classical music lovers. Includes everything from Renaissance music to Vivaldi and Mozart to Mendelssohn. Lyrics in the original language are included when appropriate.

00240044 $24.95

R&B Fake Book
This terrific fake book features more than 250 classic R&B hits: Baby Love • Best of My Love • Dancing in the Street • Easy • Get Ready • Heatwave • Here and Now • Just Once • Let's Get It On • The Loco-Motion • (You Make Me Feel Like) A Natural Woman • One Sweet Day • Papa Was a Rollin' Stone • Save the Best for Last • September • Sexual Healing • Shop Around • Smoke Gets in Your Eyes • Still • Tell It Like It Is • Up on the Roof • Walk on By • What's Going On • more!

00240107 C Edition $25.00

The Ultimate Country Fake Book – 4th Edition
This 4th edition includes even more of your favorite country hits – over 700 songs by country superstars of yesterday and today: Achy Breaky Heart (Don't Tell My Heart) • Always on My Mind • Are You Lonesome Tonight? • Boot Scootin' Boogie • Crazy • Daddy Sang Bass • Down at the Twist and Shout • Elvira • Forever and Ever, Amen • Friends in Low Places • The Gambler • Jambalaya • King of the Road • Rocky Top • Sixteen Tons • There's a Tear in My Beer • What's Forever For • Your Cheatin' Heart • and more.

00240049 $39.95

Wedding & Love Fake Book
Over 400 classic and contemporary songs, including: All for Love • All I Ask of You • Anniversary Song • Ave Maria • Can You Feel the Love Tonight • Endless Love • Forever and Ever, Amen • Forever in Love • I Wanna Be Loved • It Could Happen to You • Misty • My Heart Will Go On • So in Love • Through the Years • Vision of Love • and more.

00240041 $29.95

The Irving Berlin Fake Book
Over 150 Berlin songs, including: Alexander's Ragtime Band • Always • Blue Skies • Easter Parade • God Bless America • Happy Holiday • Heat Wave • I've Got My Love to Keep Me Warm • Puttin' on the Ritz • White Christmas • and more.

00240043 $19.95

Classic Rock Fake Book
This new fake book is a great compilation of more than 250 terrific songs of the rock era, arranged for piano, voice, guitar and all C instruments. Includes: All Right Now • American Woman • Birthday • Born to Be Wild • Brown Eyed Girl • Free Bird • Honesty • I Shot the Sheriff • I Want You to Want Me • Imagine • It's Still Rock and Roll to Me • Lay Down Sally • Layla • Magic Carpet Ride • My Generation • Rikki Don't Lose That Number • Rock and Roll All Nite • Spinning Wheel • Sweet Home Alabama • White Room • We Will Rock You • lots more!

00240108 $24.95

Gospel's Greatest Fake Book
An excellent resource for Gospel titles with over 450 songs, including: Amazing Grace • At the Cross • Behold the Lamb • Blessed Assurance • He Touched Me • Heavenly Sunlight • His Eye Is on the Sparrow • Holy Ground • How Great Thou Art • I Saw the Light • I'd Rather Have Jesus • In the Garden • Joshua (Fit the Battle of Jericho) • Just a Closer Walk with Thee • Lord, I'm Coming Home • Midnight Cry • Morning Has Broken • My Tribute • Near the Cross • The Old Rugged Cross • Precious Memories • Rock of Ages • Shall We Gather at the River? • What a Friend We Have in Jesus • and more.

00240136 $24.95

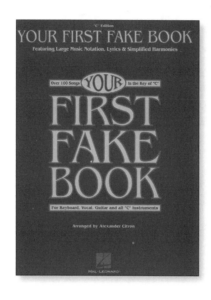
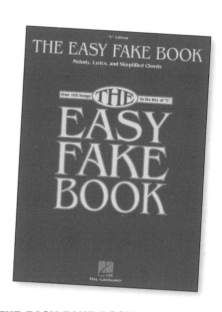

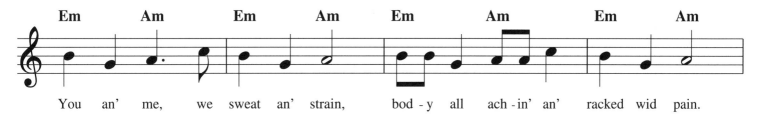

You an' me, we sweat an' strain, bod-y all ach-in' an' racked wid pain.

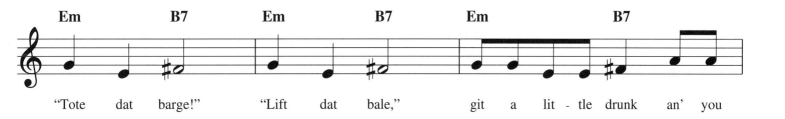

"Tote dat barge!" "Lift dat bale," git a lit-tle drunk an' you

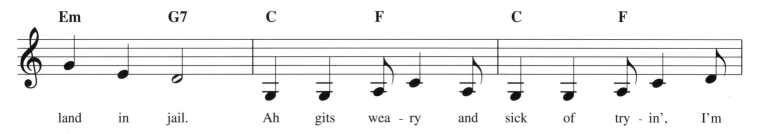

land in jail. Ah gits wea-ry and sick of try-in', I'm

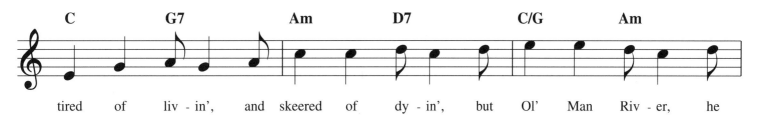

tired of liv-in', and skeered of dy-in', but Ol' Man Riv-er, he

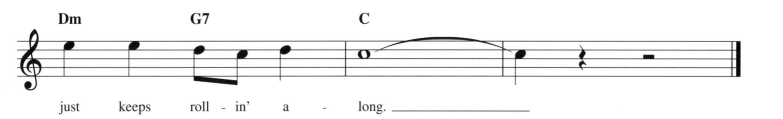

just keeps roll-in' a - long.

ON THE STREET WHERE YOU LIVE
from MY FAIR LADY

Words by ALAN JAY LERNER
Music by FREDERICK LOEWE